"Kelly has culled the vast [...] today, wrapped it around t[...] work, and produced a great contribution to the field of organizational leadership! I like the stories, the strategic perspectives, and the tactical applications built into *1-on-1 Management*™. This will be a great handbook for those that want to accelerate the people-talent war to greater victories."

Jeffrey Magee, PhD, PDM, CSP, CMC
Founder of Jeffrey Magee International
Publisher of *Performance Magazine*

"One-on-one communication creates an effective management style that is scary in its simplicity! In today's fast-paced business world, with so many management solutions available, *1-on-1 Management*™ proves to be an effective, back-to-basics approach to managing a company's most important asset—its employees. From the CEO to the entry-level manager, this book should be recommended reading for all!"

Daniel Shay, SPHR
Senior Director, Human Resources
Skanska USA Building

"*1-on-1 Management*™: *What Every Great Manager Knows That You Don't* makes sense because it teaches us things we already know to be true. It has its roots in the fundamental understanding of human motivation and inspiration. It simplifies, teaches, and facilitates true and honest communication for the purpose of developing people and high performance teams. For those CEOs and leaders who really care about their teams, their performance, and the development of their employees as well as themselves, this is a must read!"

Steve Miller, President
SCFM Compression Systems, Inc.

"Wow! I have never been so excited about a book. Riggs says all the things I have always believed but was not capable of putting into words. This is now required reading for my sales managers, and I will encourage all managers at Sunstate Equipment to read it as well. They can't have my copy though; one reading is not enough, and I will refer to it often!"

Mark Larkin, Regional Manager
Sunstate Equipment

"At our firm, we had always assumed that management consisted of preparing budgets, reviewing financial results, and handing out staff assignments, but challenges within our organization led us to understand that our management responsibilities were much greater than that.

1-on-1 Management™: What Every Great Manager Knows That You Don't provided the insight to understand that our personnel were really looking to management to help them grow and become committed to our overall goals. Learning that true leadership involves being able to communicate on a person-to-person basis has helped us to develop employees who believe in what we stand for, and has opened our eyes to identifying what we, as managers, must provide our staff in order to help them be successful.

One of the big payoffs of *1-on-1 Management™* is seeing how the individuals within our organization really blossom when given the opportunity to engage with their managers and made to feel they are an integral part of what makes our firm special."

Dan S. Cunningham, Partner
Eide Bailly, LLP

"I have brought in Kelly to speak to our company on a couple of occasions, and his performance was absolutely phenomenal! He brings a high energy and thoughtful approach that has us all wanting more. As the training coordinator for our office, it is a relief to get such great feedback every time Kelly has presented. I always look forward to bringing Kelly back; we are never disappointed! I also recommend Kelly's first book, *1-on-1 Management™: What Every Great Manager Knows That You Don't*, an excellent read that has already improved my management skills."

Kevin Lawrence, Manager
Hogan Taylor, LLP, Certified Public Accountants

"I first met Kelly Riggs when he worked with me as an executive coach. In our coaching sessions, we spent considerable time discussing relationships and how improving both my business and personal relationships would help me advance my career. Later, when *1-on-1 Management™: What Every Great Manager Knows That You Don't* was released, I had the opportunity to see how many of those relationship ideas were woven into the book.

Do not let the title fool you; this is not just a book about becoming a better manager. It is also about how to manage your personal and professional relationships and become a better person!"

Larry Straining, CPLP
Innovation and Technology Evangelist
Larry's Training, Inc.

1-on-1 Management™

**What Every Great Manager Knows
That You Don't**

1-on-1 Management™

What Every Great Manager Knows That You Don't

Kelly Riggs

1-on-1 Management™
What Every Great Manager Knows That You Don't

© 2008 Kelly Riggs
Cover design by Brent Riggs

All rights reserved. No part of this publication may be used or reproduced in any manner whatsoever without written permission except in the case of brief quotations embodied in critical articles and reviews.

Manufactured in the United States of America.

For information, please contact:

The P3 Press
16200 North Dallas Parkway, Suite 170
Dallas, Texas 75248
www.TheP3Press.com
972-381-0009

A New Era in Publishing™

ISBN-13: 978-1-933651-21-7
ISBN-10: 1-933651-21-0
LCCN: 2007941594

www.1-on-1Management.com
kelly@vmaxpg.com

Table of Contents

Foreword ix
Acknowledgments xi
Introduction xiii
1. The Path to Management. 1
2. Workplace Challenges 11
3. What Employees Really Want at Work 21
4. Introduction to 1-on-1 Management™ 35
5. Effective Communication in the Workplace 47
6. The Power of Expectations. 67
7. Four Key Questions Every Manager Must Answer (Part 1) 85
8. Four Key Questions Every Manager Must Answer (Part 2) 105
9. Creating an Environment of Employee Engagement. 119
10. The 1-on-1 Meeting™. 139
11. Coaching in the Workplace 159
12. The 1-on-1 Development Plan™. 181
13. What Every Great Manager Knows That You Don't 197
      Summary of 1-on-1 Principles™ 203
      1-on-1 Meeting™ Tips 205
Appendix A: 17 Essential Books for the Great Manager 209
Notes 211
About the Author

Foreword

In early 2009, we were in the planning and development stages of a significant corporate restructuring process at BNSF Logistics, Inc. We concluded that an outside perspective would be critical to our success, so we interviewed three consultancy firms before ultimately choosing Kelly Riggs and Vmax Performance Group to facilitate the project.

Kelly quickly proved his value to our organization, leading us efficiently through the preparation and execution phases of the restructuring assignment, but his ability to almost instantly identify with our people, our issues, and what our firm needed was truly astounding. I was particularly pleased with Kelly's capability to impact the specific restructuring project at hand while simultaneously addressing broader organizational issues.

Having identified mid-level management leadership training as an area of opportunity at BNSF Logistics, I tasked Kelly to implement the leadership development program that follows the construct of his book, *1-on-1 Management™: What Every Great Manager Knows That You Don't*. Kelly's views and teachings are relevant for all organizations, but I felt they were particularly applicable for a knowledge-based organization, like ours, that relies heavily on its people as a critical, differentiating asset.

Effective communication is critical to any organization, and *1-on-1 Management*™ teaches the importance of a consistent, weekly 1-on-1 Meeting™, with an agenda that focuses on mentoring, coaching, and personal feedback, as well as accountability to critical performance areas. A number of our mid-level managers have implemented the 1-on-1 Management™ principles and techniques, and we immediately observed quantitative improvements in how our employees relate to their managers. In my view, we are turning mid-level managers into people development specialists—a task that is critical for the longevity of our organization.

With this demonstrated success, BNSF Logistics is now going forward with 1-on-1 Management™ training throughout the company. If we can train our managers to truly improve their managerial leadership skills, we will take an already high-performance organization and unlock additional potential, elevating us to the next level of performance.

The leadership concepts that Kelly outlines in his book are easy to understand and to implement, yet are often overlooked or neglected in the daily bustle of management. I am convinced that the effective implementation of these principles will produce an immediate and positive impact on any organization!

Get ready for a thought-provoking, high-impact book that is filled with relevant examples and documented results.

Enjoy!

Eric Wolfe
Vice President & General Manager
BNSF Logistics, Inc.

Acknowledgments

In many ways, this book was a family project. Rhonda, my wife of twenty-six years, has never failed to enthusiastically support me in any project I have undertaken, and her encouragement throughout this one has been extraordinary. She is, quite simply, the best 1-on-1 Manager™ I have ever seen. This book would not have been possible without her patience, support, and feedback.

My daughter, Kristina, is the real writer in the family and she provided the initial editing for this book. She is everything a dad could ever ask for in a daughter. Thank you, Sis—I am grateful for all of your help!

I would also like to thank my two sons, Robby and Scott, for their constant inspiration and support. I thank God for allowing me to be their dad and share so many great times with them.

I have been fortunate to have my brother, Bruce, as a personal coach and sounding board for quite some time. I am indebted to him for all of his advice, which has been invaluable as I have developed my consulting business and its core curriculum.

My brother, Brent, has supplied the bulk of the graphic design for my company and for this book. I suspect that he has few equals in terms of turning creative ideas into world-class designs, and I am thankful to have access to his considerable talent.

I would also like to extend my heartfelt thanks to Jeff Magee for all of his help and encouragement as I prepared this manuscript. In the true spirit of Cavett Roberts, the founder of the National Speakers Association, Jeff has generously shared his thoughts and ideas and his advice has helped me to avoid a number of land mines as I have developed this book and my consulting business.

Finally, I want to acknowledge my faith in God and the resurrected Christ. I have been blessed in so many ways, and one of those has been to share the principles of 1-on-1 Management™, many of which are simply God's ways for treating people as presented in the Scriptures.

Introduction

Having read hundreds of books and articles on management and leadership, I suspect that the average manager—if there is such a thing—finds it difficult to discern which of the myriad of management concepts available on business bookshelves today would best suit him or her. More to the point, my experience is that these managers are often so busy with the demands of managing a business or a department that personal development is relegated to the occasional training seminar, if that.

So, why another management book? One very good reason is that the "average manager" does not work at a Fortune 500 company, but is employed in the other 99 per cent of the business landscape—small to mid-size businesses. Eighty per cent of these businesses employ fewer than one hundred employees, and rarely do they benefit from the sophisticated, and costly, corporate training and development programs that big companies enjoy. The average manager lacks the resources—and the time—to develop the managerial and leadership skills they know would improve their performance. The 1-on-1 Management™ concepts introduced in this book provide an easy-to-understand, and easy-to-implement, methodology for developing essential managerial skills.

A second reason is that the average manager isn't looking

for theories or complicated management models. What they want—indeed, what they desperately need—is a step-by-step approach to effective management that creates real results: a set of proven management principles that can be used immediately to build trust, improve communication, and create a positive work environment. 1-on-1 Management™ is such a tool.

Background

The catalyst to translate these ideas into a book came from a meeting with a client in the fall of 2006. As we reviewed a training session for the company's management team, the president of the company revealed that the real eye-opener for him was a very simple idea—meeting consistently, one-on-one, with individual employees to review activity and preview upcoming projects. While this concept is hardly revolutionary, it occurred to me that very few businesses actually engage their employees in a one-on-one fashion. At the same time, the most consistent management problem that organizations face is disengaged employees. Might there be a correlation?

While one-on-*many* meetings are a staple of the business world, I believe that trust, effective communication, and professional growth are most effectively accomplished one-on-one. It is one of the critical cornerstones of my own training and management philosophy, and one that I learned very early in my career.

David Maister, identified in the management text *Business Minds*[1] as one of the top forty business thinkers in the world, has said that "the only managerial activities worthy of the name are one-on-one; everything else is window dressing."[2] Stunning in its simplicity, this concept is a key to developing high performance teams. Indeed, I'm convinced that this is the core of what every great manager knows about management: activities, projects, and processes can be directed in a one-on-many fashion, but people management and individual development is most effectively accomplished by engaging employees one-on-one.

After twenty-five years in the business world, I can safely say that much of what I have learned has come directly from my own personal mistakes, but like you, I'm sure, I have also experienced my share of less-than-inspiring leaders. I suspect that it is the rare individual that doesn't experience a bad manager, mentor, or role model somewhere in life, but I am also convinced that these individuals serve a useful purpose in our personal development. After all, the great military leader General H. Norman Schwarzkopf once observed that you can learn as much from a bad leader as a good one! Unquestionably, though, I think we can agree that it is the truly exceptional leaders that dramatically impact and focus our careers.

Early in my business career, I was privileged to work for such a manager, a person who understood and practiced the idea of one-on-one management. A regional sales manager named Tom Corcoran hired me to work as a sales representative for Sweetheart Cup, later a division of Fort Howard Paper, and he was my introduction to what every great manager knows. When I was only twenty-three years old, Tom unwittingly laid the foundation for my business success and, as it turns out, for this book. In the time that I worked for him, he encouraged me to grow personally and professionally, took personal steps to help me do just that, and consistently engaged me in one-on-

one meetings to review my progress and establish new learning objectives.

Frankly, the success principles of effective managers are not difficult to comprehend, but, like many great business concepts, the complexity is not in the idea itself but in its execution—as we shall soon see.

The fact is most managers see the management process as akin to moving chess pieces on a board—allocating resources, assigning projects, delegating responsibilities, driving the bottom line, and, of course, conducting endless one-on-*many* meetings. The truly great manager sees most of these activities as secondary to their real responsibilities—to grow employees, unleash their potential, and construct a work environment that permits individuals to multiply their effectiveness. These high performance managers excel at identifying talent, providing the resources for success, and developing their employees' innate capabilities.

This book obviously does not make any claims to a new theory of management; it is simply a distillation of ideas that great managers—head coaches, military officers, business owners, chief executives, department heads, volunteer leaders—have always known and executed. While the simplicity of these concepts may be disarming, their successful execution requires a steadfast belief in people and their abilities—something that many managers are simply unwilling or unable to develop. Managing without trust is like asking someone to be committed to a cause without providing them with any reason whatsoever to do so.

So, what does this book offer to the reader? First, it provides a simple, but effective methodology for creating a workplace environment of trust and developing the basic people skills that characterize effective leaders. Second, it provides managers with the opportunity to dramatically improve the performance of their department or business unit as they learn to unlock the hidden potential of talented employees. Third, the concepts presented here help alleviate a great deal of the stress associated with managing people. In understanding the employee's perspective of the workplace, managers will learn to lead employees in a positive and proactive way that will create an atmosphere of commitment and accountability.

Our journey begins by looking at the traditional path to management that dominates the business landscape (chapter 1), and then we will explore the reasons that a significant percentage of employees are disconnected, disengaged, and disinterested in driving corporate objectives (chapter 2). Next, we will discover what employees really want—in fact, desperately need—to become engaged and productive in the workplace (chapter 3). Then, I will introduce the concepts of 1-on-1 Management™ (chapter 4), before discussing the critical importance of communication in effective management (chapters 5 through 8). The remainder of the book will be dedicated to outlining the simple, yet profound, 1-on-1 Management™ principles that great managers utilize successfully.

Engaging employees one-on-one and learning the principles of developing talent will put you in a league of your own as a manager. It is a sad reminder of the far distant industrial age, where most modern management principles were first developed, that many managers still see themselves as the boss that barks out orders, demands respect and obedience, and thrashes those that fall short of perfection.

It is my hope that this book will challenge you to see 1-on-1 Management™ as an effective way to build a vibrant and productive company, business unit, or department. These concepts may be more difficult than simply issuing ultimatums and demanding compliance, but managers generally agree that a company or department can only be as good as the individuals on the team. With that in mind, it follows that growing those individuals is the key to a high performance organization.

A simple concept, yes, but one that requires a wise and talented manager to execute it successfully.

Perhaps that is why great managers are so rare.

The Path to Management

Management: the process of getting things done through other people

"So much of what we call management consists of making it difficult for people to work."

—Peter Drucker

Even in this age of advanced technology, where the distribution of knowledge far outstrips our ability to absorb it, there is a deep chasm between the understanding of what management is and what its practical applications are in the workplace. We do not have to look far to find the origins of this misunderstanding. Consider this definition of "management":

> Management (from Old French *ménagement,* "the art of conducting, directing;" from Latin *manu agere,* "to lead by the hand"): characterizes the process of leading and directing all or part of an organization, often a business, through the deployment and manipulation of resources (human, financial, material, intellectual, or intangible)[3]

1-on-1 Management

Of course! Management is about conducting or directing! Can you visualize yourself as a manager in front of a group of employees, telling them when to "play" and when to stop? How softly and at what tempo? An orchestra responding to your every whim. Or, can you see yourself "directing" those employees? When to speak and which lines to use? What emotions to display and how to act out the scene just so? A cast of characters waiting for your next cue.

Worse, though, is this idea of employees as "human" resources to be manipulated, alongside financial, material, intellectual, and intangible resources. Employees are viewed as chess pieces to be deployed: sacrificing a pawn to save a knight, or moving a rook across the board to pin the queen. This approach treats human beings as resources to expend or allocate as needed—exactly like raw materials or financial instruments.

It is interesting to note the Latin etymology of the word management: manu agere, "to lead by the hand." Here, we find a sense of the word that includes people in ways other than as pawns or players. While "leading by the hand" may conjure up images of teaching children, the idea extends deeper than we first perceive. Leading by the hand implies trust. It implies caring and understanding. It implies teaching and learning—until the individual reaches the point of no longer needing to be taught.

To be sure, managers "manage" processes in the course of work, but in the final analysis managers are responsible for getting things done through people. Period. To be effective with people, managers must learn a set of skills that enable them to build trust, forge relationships, teach and coach, and communicate effectively.

Assessing Managers

Ask any employee to describe or assess his or her manager and the odds are pretty good that you will get an answer deserving of an "R" rating. Although you may occasionally get exactly the opposite—a glowing review suitable for framing—employee surveys support the notion that managers as a whole are not exactly held in the highest esteem. According to a 2005 Conference Board Report, less than one-third of all supervisors and managers were perceived to be strong leaders.[4]

Less than one in three. A one-in-three batting average may get you in the Baseball Hall of Fame, but as a business owner, one-in-three effective managers will get you broke in a hurry.

Why do employees have such a poor view of managers? I am certain there are a number of variables to consider—competence, integrity, personalities, dependability, etc.—but I suspect that the most compelling factor is likely the ability (or more accurately, the inability) to deal with people. People skills. What author Daniel Goleman calls "emotional intelligence," or being intelligent about emotions.[5] In his book, *Primal Leadership: Realizing the Power of Emotional Intelligence*, Goleman states:

> Emotional self-awareness creates leaders who are authentic, able to give advice that is genuinely in the employee's best interest rather than advice that leaves the person feeling manipulated or even attacked. And empathy means leaders listen first before reacting or giving feedback, which allows the interaction to stay on target.[6]

Emotional self-awareness? I will wager that the typical management promotion decision does not consider this particular competency, but look closely at what Goleman is describing: "the employee's best interest," "empathy," and "listen first before reacting" are, quite simply, *people skills*. These are the skills that allow managers to connect with employees and understand their needs. These leaders develop trust because they value people and actively cultivate the skills to create that trust.

These are the skills that managers don't have, fail to develop, or simply do not care about. We will look more closely at what employees really need in the workplace in chapter 3 but for now, it will suffice to say that they don't seem to be getting much of it. Only one-third of supervisors and managers are perceived to be strong leaders. Read between the lines: if the supervisors and managers aren't strong leaders, we may rightly conclude that their employees aren't willing to follow them.

Management Qualifications

It is pretty absurd when you think about it, but a significant percentage of managers assume their new responsibilities without any meaningful training in the principles of people management. Frankly, as I talk to managers about how they reached their position, I find that it usually has little to do with the ability to lead, manage, or develop people, but is likely the result of other common factors or circumstances. Most frequently, managers are chosen from the ranks of achievers or from those with highly developed knowledge or skills. While it is true that a manager should be competent, if not superlative,

The Path to Management

in the skills and/or knowledge necessary to work in their area of responsibility, does it necessarily follow that this individual will necessarily become an effective and successful manager?

My own experience is exemplary of the process through which one is typically promoted to management. In November 1987, and I was hired by an orthopedic products company based in northern California to be their sales representative for Oklahoma, Missouri, and Arkansas. After fourteen months of struggling to learn the company's products and build relationships with orthopedic surgeons in three states, I finally hit my stride in December 1986, finishing the month as the top sales representative in the company.

The momentum continued into 1987 and I finished the year as the No. 1 sales representative in the country, setting a couple of sales records in the process and, more importantly for me, achieving the top level of the coveted President's Club Award for the first time in the company's history. The recognition for being No. 1 was terrific, but the President's Club Award also included an all-expenses paid vacation to Hawaii. Thanks, boss!

The following year, I repeated as the top sales rep in the country—this time sharing the top slot with a good friend, an incredibly talented sales rep in Colorado—and once again, I achieved the top level of the President's Club. Then, early in 1989, the company did what most companies tend to do when they need a manager—they offered to promote me, a top producer, to an open management position.

1st Question: Other than being a top sales performer, what were my qualifications to fill a role that required me to manage several people?

1-on-1 Management

2nd Question: How much training did the company provide to develop me as a sales manager?

Answer to both questions: Zip.

What is telling in my circumstance is the conversation I had with the owner of the company two years later. He told me that he didn't really know if I would make a good manager, but he thought I deserved the opportunity. This is, in fact, the norm for small and medium-sized businesses. While we may not be sure if an individual can or will be a good manager, we believe that their achievement, knowledge, or skills should allow them the opportunity to "move up."

Understand that I am not asserting that a high achiever or technical wizard can't or won't be a good manager. I am simply pointing out that people development skills have to be learned like any other, and they are absolutely necessary to management success. In my experience, it is not at all uncommon for the opportunity to "move up" to turn into a disaster, with the frustrated manager returning to the employee ranks or, worse, leaving the company.

College Degrees Don't Seem to Help

OK, so you have identified an individual in the organization that you would like to promote to management, and to your great delight, you learn that he or she has a college degree in a business-related field! Obviously, this candidate will have a solid grasp of management fundamentals, right?

Think again.

In college you are taught extensively about what management is; but how to be a manager? Forget it.

The Path to Management

The typical college text describes the functions of a manager as planning, organizing, leading, and controlling—a lovely word for managing people, don't you think? These texts contain a detailed description of the origins of modern management principles, followed by expansive discussions of current thought regarding those four functions. So, the student is led to understand what management is about and is exposed to various ideas about planning systems, organizational theory, leadership concepts, and control mechanisms, but absolutely nothing about how to *become* an effective manager. The student will rarely, if ever, delve into the books or materials that will provide them with some understanding of the real tools necessary to successfully manage people.[8]

How about a business school graduate? Great management material, wouldn't you think? Henry Mintzberg, Cleghorn Professor of Management Studies at McGill University in Montreal and author of the 2003 book *Managers, Not MBAs*, is considered one of the world's best-known management scholars.[9] In an interview with the *Conference Board Review*, Mintzberg observed that:

> The typical business school today is concerned with business functions, not management. Certainly managers have to understand business functions—marketing, accounting, sales, and so on—but the practice of business is not the same as the practice of management. Mixing all these functions together in a person is not going to produce a manager.[10]

An astonishing insight, to be sure. Concerning those MBA graduates, Mintzberg adds, "There's not much evidence that these people have managerial skills or even that they truly want to be managers."[11]

Great! We are left to conclude that, generally speaking, neither college degrees nor business schools adequately prepare an individual to manage people. Manage business functions? Yes. Manage core processes? Sure. Manage people? Not so much.

Conclusion

Interacting with managers of different levels of responsibility in several industries, I have consistently heard the same complaint voiced over and over again: "I know how to do the technical aspects of my job very well, but I have never been trained in how to deal effectively with employees." Many managers seem to clearly recognize the challenges they face in balancing performance expectations against employee satisfaction, but few have any idea as to how they should address those challenges.

This is the reality of most managers: having worked extremely hard to be recognized and promoted for their accomplishments or specialized technical skills, they will almost automatically (in the absence of training) continue to derive their own personal value in the company from those "qualifications"—answering questions, solving problems, and becoming the technical "go-to" person in the department. This sense of being "in charge"—dispensing answers, resolving problems, directing traffic—makes a manager feel needed and valued, but fails to capture the potential of the employees or develop the full capacity of the team!

In fact, it creates a predictable and significant bottleneck in workplace productivity, since team members consistently fail

The Path to Management

to develop their own problem solving skills (we certainly can't have employees making mistakes, can we?), and employees learn not to act without managerial approval. While this may describe nirvana for the enthusiastic micro-manager, otherwise talented and capable employees become dependent on the resident expert, the manager, for completion of difficult or challenging assignments.

The end-result of this scenario is a distrust that slowly seeps into the organization and erodes it from within.

1-on-1 Insights™

- Management is about leading people. Period. Your technical skills were valuable in your previous position and they will be valuable as a manager, but the reason you were promoted was to manage people.

- People management is a skill that must be learned; it doesn't come gift-wrapped alongside your achievements or with the development of specialized knowledge or skills.

- Solving problems is a useful *skill* for a manager; developing employees and empowering them to think for themselves is real management.

Workplace Challenges 2

Influence: the power of producing a desired effect in an indirect or intangible way

> "I believe the real difference between success and failure in a corporation can be very often traced to the question of how well the organization brings out the great energies and talents of its people."
>
> —Thomas J. Watson, Jr.

Leadership is influence.

So says John Maxwell, a recognized leadership authority and successful author (twelve million books sold).

So says Kenneth Blanchard, author of *One Minute Manager* (seven million copies sold).

So says Stephen Covey, author of *7 Habits of Highly Effective People* (fifteen million copies sold).

Get the picture? By just about anyone's definition, leadership is influence.

Let's take a closer look at the definition of influence: *the power of producing an effect in an indirect way.*[12] Doesn't that sound a whole lot like what managers do? It sounds like "getting things done (*producing an effect*) through other people (*in an indirect way*)," wouldn't you agree?

In fact, introductory management texts teach that one of the primary components of management is leadership, along with the functions of planning, organizing, and controlling. While there are pundits who assert that managing and leading are two different things, Management 101 at any college or university teaches us that leadership is a component part of the management process. Although a leader may not necessarily manage people, we can safely say that managers *are* leaders so long as they have any responsibility for employees!

So, what is the point? Since leadership is influence and managers are necessarily leaders, we can rightly conclude that management is influence—the power of producing an effect in an indirect or intangible way. *The question is, how much training does the average manager receive in the skills of developing influence?* Evidently, not nearly enough, at least from the employee's perspective. According to a 2005 Conference Board Report, employee workplace satisfaction continues to decline at an alarming rate. Consider these findings:

- Only 50 percent of workers were satisfied with their jobs in 2004, compared to 60 percent in 1995.

- 40 percent of workers feel disconnected from their employers.

- Two out of three employees are not motivated to drive their employer's business goals.

- 25 percent are just showing up to collect a check.[13]

Workplace Challenges

According to this report, employees are increasingly disconnected, disengaged, and disinterested in the company's business objectives. The important, and logical, question to ask is "Why?" Why are employees disengaged? Is there a common factor that creates the dismal picture painted by these statistics?

I believe there is a common factor, and I believe the study clearly answers both of our questions for us. This is the same study in which employees reported that only one out of three managers is considered to be effective leader. There is your answer—clear, concise, and easy-to-understand. How common is it for members of *any* organization to produce great results for a poor leader? How satisfying or rewarding is it to work in any organization—of any kind—that has poor leadership? Poor leadership eventually results in disengaged, disinterested, and poor performing organizations.

Now consider your own company or department. What is the impact on your workplace productivity if two out of three employees in your company are not motivated to drive your business goals? As we discussed in chapter 1, today's managers not only find themselves in a role for which they may not be adequately prepared, but they may also be given responsibility for a group of employees who couldn't care less about the success of the company.

It gets worse. While disengaged employees represent a huge drain on workplace productivity, those costs multiply when employees leave the company and must be replaced. Employee retention is now a significant workplace issue—one that will continue to grow in importance. A 2005 Emerging Workforce Study compiled by recruiting and staffing firm Spherion, revealed the following:

- Only 44 percent of U.S. workers believe their companies are taking steps to retain them, and 31 percent believe there is a turnover problem at their company already.

- Only 34 percent of HR managers mention turnover/retention as a key HR concern.

- While employers expect only 14 percent of their workers to leave the company in the next year, nearly 40 percent of U.S. workers indicate their intention to find a new job in the next twelve months.[14]

With so much at stake, what is your company doing now to prepare? As the competition for top employee talent increases, it is not at all inconceivable that savvy competitors will target your critical employees and key leaders and lure them to a workplace that is more fulfilling, more rewarding, and more conducive to personal growth. What would the loss of several key employees do to your ability to compete effectively in the marketplace?

In 2002, the *MIT Sloan Management Review* published the following in an article entitled "Building Competitive Advantage through People":

There is a surplus of capital chasing a scarcity of talented people and the knowledge they possess. In today's economy, that is the constraining—and therefore strategic—resource.[15]

Geoffrey Colvin, senior editor of *Fortune* magazine, agrees: "After five hundred years or so, the scarcest, most valuable resource in business is no longer financial capital. It's talent."[16]

One thing is certain—the labor climate is unlikely to change any time soon. While it is hard enough to find and attract talented employees today, according to Bureau of Labor statistics, employment opportunities will outstrip available workers to the tune of ten million jobs by 2010.[17]

Leadership Defines an Organization

As we have discussed, managers are quite often placed into management roles with little or no leadership training, and employees are increasingly judging those managers to be ineffective. One of the first realities that a company must face is that *managers* are often the critical factor in the problems discussed above.

> **1-on-1 Principle™:** Employees join companies, but they leave managers.

One ineffective, poorly prepared manager can have a devastating effect on an otherwise excellent company, not the least of which is the loss of talented employees. Best-selling authors Marcus Buckingham and Curt Coffman echo this idea in the book *First, Break All the Rules:*

> People leave managers, not companies. So much money has been thrown at the challenge of keeping good people—in the form of better pay, better perks, and better training—when, in the end, turnover is mostly a manager issue.[18]

1-on-1 Management

Talk to an employee that is looking for greener pastures and they will often tell you they are simply searching for a "good company" or a "better company." Further conversation will often reveal the presence of a manager that did not know how to deal with people. In fact, a "good company" really means a "good manager" to most individuals. While there are dozens of reasons that talented people leave companies, more often than not, it has little to do with the work, the benefits, or even the pay. It is a failure of the manager—a failure to inspire; a failure to communicate; a failure to create opportunity; a failure to value employee contributions; a failure to develop potential. These failures ultimately influence the employee to pursue fulfillment elsewhere.

What is apparent is that *leadership defines an organization*. The hallmark of a strong, vibrant company is usually a cadre of strong, empathetic, people-focused leaders, while struggling companies will often have self-centered, arrogant, or hyper-critical leaders. Jim Collins describes it this way in *Good to Great*:

> The moment a leader allows himself to become the primary reality people worry about, rather than reality being the primary reality, you have a recipe for mediocrity, or worse.[19]

A leader defines the organization by either becoming the "primary reality people worry about" or by making reality the primary reality. Translation? The priorities in an organization are determined by the leader, whether the top priority is him/her or something else. As a result, the people in any organizational unit will almost always be a fairly accurate reflection of the leader.

Workplace Challenges

After all, *people generally tend to do what is expected of them*, don't they? If the boss is critical, the employees are typically averse to risk or making decisions and they are often just as critical of others. If the boss is sensitive to people, the employees will often exhibit the same behavior. The average owner or manager tends to choose employees that share similar personalities and character traits.

Prove it to yourself. With few exceptions, I think you can spend five or ten minutes with the people in just about any business office or department and probably get a good grasp of what the boss is like and what he or she considers to be important. For example, if you can't find anyone to help you in a retail store (or worse, you are just being ignored), chances are pretty good the boss doesn't have very high expectations for customer service. Instead of focusing on the customer, you may find the employees diligently stocking shelves or doing other busy work, oblivious to the needs of the customer. These actions, more often than not, reflect the business priorities mandated to the employee by the owner or manager rather than the decision of the employee.

1-on-1 Principle™: Organizations will directly reflect the values and personality of the leader.

Your leadership—as a manager, owner, or executive—defines your organization. Your people are a reflection of you. Whatever is important to you will be important to them. *Look carefully at what motivates you, and you will probably see it in your organization.* If you are highly critical, your staff will most likely operate out of fear and hesitate to solve problems for your customers. If you tend to accept mediocre work from one employee, you will probably see mediocrity creep into the organization as your staff realizes that excellence is not expected or rewarded. Worse yet, if you demand one set of behaviors and reward a different set of behaviors, the workplace will constantly be in turmoil.

So, if employees are generally dissatisfied with their jobs and disinterested in your company's business objectives, whose fault is it?

Three hints: Who hired them? Who trained them? Who leads them?

Conclusion

Perhaps one of the most pervasive comments heard from managers and business owners is that employees just don't have any "commitment" to the company. The reasons ascribed to this problem usually boil down to something like the following: "Generation X or Y or Z (or MTV, or whatever the appropriate label) just isn't motivated," or "you just can't find good employees any more." From this perspective, the lack of commitment is the employee's fault and is caused by a lack of motivation or an entitlement mentality or something similar.

Certainly, the evidence suggests that there is some truth to this idea. After all, the Conference Board statistics detailed above certainly seem to outline a lack of employee commitment. However, the real issue is not really whether the employee is or is not committed to the company but who is ultimately responsible for the lack of commitment?

Here is the bottom line: good employees are difficult to

Workplace Challenges

find, and ineffective managers are putting those employees at risk. Great managers, however, know how to attract, retain, and develop talented employees, and that is the silver lining in this scenario. Companies that solve the riddle of employee satisfaction will have a distinct competitive advantage in the marketplace! When owners or managers can accurately determine what really motivates employees to become committed to the company's mission, vision, and values, they will be in the enviable position of being able to positively influence employees and unleash their potential.

For now, we can safely assert that managers are mostly failing with employees: failing to effectively lead, failing to exert positive influence, and failing to communicate a compelling vision that motivates employees to drive business goals.

In the next chapter, we will undertake the mission of finding out what *really* motivates employees.

1-on-1 Insights™

- Management is influence. To be a good manager, one must learn and develop the skills that develop the capacity to influence employees.

- If employees are disconnected and disengaged, take a closer look at the company's management—at all levels.

- A single ineffective manager can compromise your competitive advantages and negate your most important strategic asset—talented employees.

- Leadership defines an organization. Good, bad, or non-existent, organizations reflect the influence of their leaders.

What Employees Really Want at Work

A committed employee is motivated by shared purpose.
A compliant employee is motivated by fear.

> "The deepest craving in human nature is the craving to be appreciated."
>
> —William James (1842-1910)

One under-performing employee has the capacity to derail the most resourceful organization. Companies with innovative products and services, state-of-the-art facilities, overflowing advertising budgets, and even the very finest customer support systems, can be sorely compromised by disengaged or disconnected employees.

Typically, there are two solutions to this problem.

The first is to simply replace an employee with a more talented one. No arguments here, if talent is truly the issue. There is no doubt that an organization can never be what its employees are not. Mediocre employees make for a mediocre company. The only question here is whether or not the employee is the real issue.

1-on-1 Management

The second is to tighten the screws: more controls, more rules, more management oversight. This approach will get you plenty of argument from me. This tactic might produce some short-term gains—maybe—but the long-term damage to the organization may be irreversible. Why? Talented employees do not want to be micro-managed, and you cannot get the maximum performance out of employees by dictating every behavior. They will eventually leave—or worse.

If you believe that tighter controls and rigid, inflexible rules produce more productive employees, I would suggest that you have your head in the sand or your sense of value as a manager is found in barking orders and demanding compliance. I would also suggest that it makes little sense to do more of exactly what created the problem in the first place. Disengagement is a condition that is created, not one that exists. Show me a company full of disengaged employees, and I will show you an organization whose leaders have created the problem. Every time.

There is, of course, a third solution to disengaged employees, and that is to hire or train managers who understand how to engage employees. The evidence in the workplace is simply overwhelming—companies cannot lower costs, improve quality, super-serve the customer, or create innovative solutions over the long term without committed, engaged, and enthusiastic employees.

In fact, Jack Welch's success as CEO at General Electric was in very large part due to his personnel strategy: to hire the very best employees, give them a mission, and get out of the way. *Business Week* shared his story in 1998:

Less well understood, however, is how Jack Welch (was) able to wield so much *influence* [italics mine] and power over the most far-flung, complex organization in all of American business. Many managers struggle daily to lead and motivate mere handfuls of people. Many CEOs wrestle to squeeze just average performance from companies a fraction of GE's size. How does Welch, who sits atop a business empire with $304 billion in assets, $89.3 billion in sales, and 276,000 employees scattered in more than 100 countries around the globe, do it?

He does it through sheer force of personality, coupled with an unbridled passion for winning the game of business and a keen attention to details many chieftains would simply overlook. He does it because he encourages near-brutal candor in the meetings he holds to guide the company through each work year. *And he does it because, above all else, he's a fierce believer in the power of his people* [italics mine]."[20]

What few people know about Welch is his own early experience as an engineer with General Electric. Over forty years ago, Welch had decided to leave GE—for exactly the reasons we discussed in the previous chapter:

John Francis Welch Jr. had worked for General Electric not much more than a year when in 1961 he abruptly quit his $10,500 job as a junior engineer in Pittsfield, Mass. He felt stifled by the company's bureaucracy, underappreciated by his boss, and offended by the civil service-style $1,000 raise he was given. Welch wanted out, and to get out he had accepted a job offer from International Minerals & Chemicals in Skokie, Ill.

1-on-1 Management

But Reuben Gutoff, then a young executive a layer up from Welch, had other ideas. He had been mightily impressed by the young upstart and was shocked to hear of his impending departure and farewell party just two days away. Desperate to keep him, Gutoff coaxed Welch and his wife, Carolyn, out to dinner that night. For four straight hours at the Yellow Aster in Pittsfield, he made his pitch: Gutoff swore he would prevent Welch from being entangled in GE red tape and vowed to create for him a small-company environment with big-company resources. These were themes that would later dominate Welch's own thinking as CEO.

"Trust me," Gutoff remembers pleading. "As long as I am here, you are going to get a shot to operate with the best of the big company and the worst part of it pushed aside."

"Well, you are on trial," retorted Welch.

"I'm glad to be on trial," Gutoff said. "To try to keep you here is important."[21]

If not for Reuben Gutoff—an unsung middle manager who understood what employees need to reach their potential and find fulfillment in the workplace—Jack Welch would have been lost to GE.

What Do Employees Want?

Let's dispense with the obvious answer first. Employees want to be paid well. They also want excellent benefits. Without question, those two things are written in bedrock. In fact, if you look at any number of employee surveys across all industries, compensation and benefits are most often the two most important items with regard to employee job satisfaction.

However, a word of caution—this data, in a vacuum, can be misleading.

When employees are asked to take surveys on items that relate to their personal job satisfaction, they are instructed to score each of them—things like compensation, benefits, job security, challenging work, relationship with the manager, etc.—on a scale of 1 to 5 (or, using five degrees of importance, ranging from very unimportant to very important). Using this survey methodology, compensation and benefits will almost universally be ranked as "very important". After all, don't we all want to get paid? Aren't good benefits and good pay *very important*?

Every year for the last five years, the Society for Human Resource Management (SHRM) has published their Job Satisfaction Survey Report identifying the top job satisfaction indicators. Each year, benefits and compensation are ranked by nearly two out of three employees surveyed as "very important", and were the top two factors in job satisfaction, respectively, in 2005.[22]

David Sirota, author of *The Enthusiastic Employee: How Companies Profit by Giving Employees What They Want*, confirmed the importance of employee compensation and benefits in an interview with Knowledge@Wharton in 2005:

> We find there are three basic goals of people at work. First, to be treated fairly. We call that equity. Employees want to know they are getting fair pay, which is normally defined as

competitive pay. They want benefits and job security. These days, employees especially need medical benefits, so those have become significant.[23]

I seriously doubt that anyone would fail to see the necessity of respectable compensation when considering an employee's job satisfaction. However, a potential problem is that many employers tend to think that compensation is the *only* issue that relates to job satisfaction.

It is also noteworthy to examine the methodology of the typical job satisfaction survey. Each item in the survey is rated completely independent of the others factors. In other words, all twenty-one items in the SHRM Job Satisfaction Survey could theoretically be rated "very important" to the employee. But what would the results be if each item had to be ranked against each other—from 1 (most important to my job satisfaction) to twenty-one (least important to my job satisfaction)?

Other Considerations

Of course, the 2005 SHRM Job Satisfaction survey reveals other factors that are "very important" to employee job satisfaction. For instance, six out of ten employees in the SHRM survey rated "Flexibility to Balance Work and Life Issues" as being "very important" and third overall in importance to job satisfaction. "Job Security" and "Feeling Safe in the Work Environment" finished fourth and fifth respectively in terms of job satisfaction.[24]

In 2004, the Stanford Graduate School of Business published research demonstrating that even graduating MBAs look beyond compensation (maybe they can afford to) when considering job satisfaction:

> Intellectual challenge topped the list as the most important attribute for MBAs in their job choice decision. Interestingly enough, the financial package was only 80 percent as important as intellectual challenge.
>
> Even more surprising was that reputation for ethics and caring about employees both rose to the top third of the list of 14 attributes, proving to be approximately 77 percent as important as the top criterion of intellectual challenge. Moreover, more than 97 percent of the MBAs in the sample said they were willing to forgo financial benefits to work for an organization with a better reputation for corporate social responsibility and ethics.[25]

Intellectual challenge, reputation for ethics, caring about employees—these are items that MBAs were willing to forego part of their salary to obtain. From one industry to another, from one position to another, from one pay grade to another—there are likely a number of items that would be considered important or very important when measuring job satisfaction.

Thus, it is evident that there are significant dynamics in play with regard to employee job satisfaction that extend well beyond compensation and benefits. Although employers should never lose sight of the importance of pay, it is clear that the factors that contribute to employee job satisfaction are more complex than we might first believe.

As I alluded to earlier, there is a very different type of survey that will generate a much different perspective on motivating employees.

What Do Employees Really Want?

In 1946, the Labor Relations Institute of New York surveyed employees to determine what was important to them at work, but unlike the SHRM survey, they asked that the following ten items be ranked in order of importance from one (most important) to ten (least important). Here are the results:

What Employees Want at Work

1. Full appreciation for work done.
2. Feeling "in" on things.
3. Sympathetic help on personal problems.
4. Job security.
5. Good wages.
6. Interesting work.
7. Promotion/growth opportunities.
8. Personal loyalty to workers.
9. Good working conditions.
10. Tactful discipline.[26]

Look very closely at this list. The first three items are profoundly revealing. If we could step outside of the workplace for a moment, we would recognize these things as simply generic human needs. Employees want to be appreciated or valued for their contributions. They want to know what is going on and feel like they are a part of things, and they want people to understand that life outside of work has an impact on their attitude and work performance.

At least that was so in 1946. Sixty years ago. But a few things have changed in that time span, don't you know? Personal computers, wireless phones, Blackberry and Bluetooth, flex-time, the Family Medical Leave Act. This is a new era, with completely new challenges. Right?

Not so much. This particular survey has been replicated several times—in the '80s, the '90s, and most recently in 2001—with almost identical results.[27] Big surprise. People are people, and it is unlikely that basic human needs are going to change much. Even in today's workplace, with all of the technology we could possibly imagine, we still have basic needs. To be valued. To be appreciated. To be listened to.

By the way, compensation is fifth on this list—high enough to be important, as I mentioned earlier. Employees definitely care about getting paid. The interesting fact is that employers were surveyed as well and given the same list of items to rank, but they ranked compensation as the most important element in employee job satisfaction. They ranked the first two items—those most important to employees—at eighth and ninth, respectively.

1-on-1 Principle™: Employees are human beings. They never lose the need to feel valued, to be recognized, and to be encouraged.

Some employers, however, have gotten the message. One good example is Chuck Knight, CEO of St. Louis-based Emer-

1-on-1 Management

son Electric from 1973 to 2000. During his tenure as chief executive, he led Emerson through the second half of an almost unprecedented business winning streak—forty-three consecutive years of annual increases in earnings per share and dividends per share. In 2006, *McKinsey Quarterly* interviewed Knight and asked him specifically what actions a company should take to retain talented employees:

> Make it hard for them to leave. At Emerson, part of that is finding opportunities for people—for example, challenging jobs in other divisions.
>
> But the environment here is really the key to retention, and I wish I could explain it better. We're a demanding company, but we're fair. I mean, I could be pretty tough with a group in a planning conference but then have dinner and drinks with them afterward, and nobody would remember how tough the discussion was. It wasn't personal, nobody got fired, and the next day everybody was working to get the plan on track.
>
> We really do care about our people. We worry about them. For example, we do a survey every two years to gauge the attitudes of our employees. We do this everywhere, at every plant, for hourly employees as well as salaried. And we track the results. If there are bad managers or supervisors out there, it shows up and we either fix the problem or get rid of them. If there's an issue, we see it and deal with it. That's one reason why very few of our plants are unionized—our employees are satisfied.[28]

The Role of Management

Knight recognized that managers play a critical role in employee retention. Management issues—specifically, people management issues—are vital to the success of a company. As we have asserted, people join companies, but they leave managers. Undoubtedly, companies throughout the nation watched bewildered as talented employees leave for competitors, discovering too late that the problem is not the employee, but the employee's manager.

The traditional approach to managing people, sometimes described as the "command and control" model, is steeped in the ancient history of management practices developed near the dawn of the industrial age, when employees were often asked to complete only one basic function or task. Employees were ecstatic to have a job, even a boring, repetitive one. Compliance as a means of motivation was effective for a simple reason—to lose a job meant going hungry.

The ensuing development of management techniques revolved around time-and-motion studies, improvements in efficiencies, and other strategies to improve productivity. Universally, these concepts were recognized as important and necessary steps in the development of business management, but today's workplace and today's employees are a far cry from the Ford plant in the early twentieth century.

In 1997, Margaret Wheatley, author of *Leadership and the New Science*, published a compelling article regarding changes in management techniques:

We have known for nearly half a century that self-managed teams are far more productive than any other form of organizing. There is a clear correlation between participation and productivity; in fact, productivity gains in truly self-managed work environments are at minimum 35 percent higher than in traditionally managed organizations.[29]

With evidence of a "clear correlation" between employee participation and dramatic improvements in employee performance, why isn't corporate America rushing to make organizational changes? Ms. Wheatley answers this way:

> . . . (control) mechanisms seem to derive from our fear—our fear of one another, of a harsh competitive world, and of the natural processes of growth and change that confront us daily. Years of such fear have resulted in these byzantine systems. We never effectively control people with these systems, but we certainly stop a lot of good work from getting done.[30]

Conclusion

The root causes for ineffective managers and disenfranchised employees are mostly systemic, with the blame resting squarely on the flawed process that routinely puts people into management slots without adequate preparation or training. Companies need managers to be sure, but to prosper in an increasingly unforgiving marketplace, companies need those managers to be strong *leaders*. Without adequate training in people development, managers are handicapped in their capacity to reach their own potential, much less the potential of those that work for them.

However, savvy managers recognize what got them promoted in the first place—specialized knowledge, highly developed skills, or capabilities that produced results for the company. Therefore, their management style will typically reflect that strength. Think about the general impression that people have of what managers do. Don't we generally visualize a manager as a decision maker, the person who provides answers, the one person in the department who can solve the problems encountered on the job? Rather than building the capabilities of the team or department, most new managers will simply continue to assert the skills and knowledge that got them recognized in the first place. It is not uncommon for the new manager to derive his or her own personal value from being a "super-technician," the person with all of the answers.

The fallout from this all-too-common situation is that talented employees get bored and search for avenues to develop their latent potential, which leads to turnover, or worse. It is not uncommon for these disengaged employees to become the nexus for dissension and turmoil in the workplace.

While talented employees are already scarce, it is only going to get worse. Several industries (banking, accounting, and healthcare, for example) have already begun to feel the effects of too few trained professionals, and it will likely become a strategic concern for many more sectors in the near future.

The good news is that talented employees are starving for a place to work that will allow them to maximize their capabilities. If companies will train their managers to develop the skills that build trust, develop potential, and create a positive work

1-on-1 Management

culture, they will create a strategic advantage that is very difficult to duplicate. That is what this book was designed to do: give managers a crash course in developing real-world, 1-on-1 Management™ skills.

Let's get started.

1-on-1 Insights™

- Command-and-control management is dated and largely ineffective. Your competitors don't want you to figure this out. It is better for them if your talented employees join their workforce.

- Compensation and benefits are important to employees. Very important. But in the final analysis, there are more important things.

- Employees need to be appreciated, listened to, and valued. Learn to do this effectively and you won't have problems keeping talented employees.

Introduction to 1-on-1 Management™

Employee engagement is directly proportional to a manager's engagement skills

"All workplace practices should be evaluated by a simple criterion: Do they convey and create trust, or do they signify distrust and destroy trust and respect among people?"

—Jeffrey Pfeffer,
The Human Equation: Building Profits by Putting People First

In the film *U-571*, actor Matthew McConaughey plays Executive Officer Lieutenant Andrew Tyler in a dramatic story about a daring mission to capture a German encryption device during World War II. After Tyler and his crew have located the device and taken control of the German submarine U-571, a battle with another German sub ensues that damages their vessel. Pursued by a German destroyer that is pounding the sea with depth charges, Tyler suddenly finds himself in command after his captain is killed. With limited maneuvering capabilities and only a single torpedo left to fight with, he is forced to take the sub to a depth of two hundred meters in order to escape. This decision leaves the crew in a dreadful situation—the sub, never designed to operate at that depth, is mere seconds from being crushed by the sea, while the only alternatives are to be destroyed by depth charges or to surface and be hammered by the destroyer's big guns.

Admittedly, managers today rarely, if ever, face life-or-death decisions. However, they are often confronted with two incompatible choices that create enormous stress. Should I maintain the current course, reacting to one crisis after another, and continue to work longer hours just to keep up? Or, should I change course entirely and attempt to develop the capabilities of my employees—who, frankly, appear disinterested and disengaged? Will the ground that I lose put my own job at risk?

In a work environment where two out of three managers are considered to be poor leaders and 50 percent of employees are unhappy, there can be incredible amounts of stress on the job—for both managers and employees. The objective of 1-on-1 Management™ is to create an environment that engages employees, satisfies the employees' need to be valued, and establishes a lasting trust between managers and employees. Unquestionably, this is a tall order—one that will require a significant investment of time and energy by a manager who most likely doesn't feel there is enough time in the day to finish the current workload. However, what is the alternative?

According to a Gallup Organization study, 56 percent of the U.S. workforce is "disengaged." These employees are in neutral and going nowhere fast, and though they aren't necessarily hurting their companies, their productivity is nowhere near what it could be if those same employees were actively engaged. Perhaps more disturbing is the study's revelation that an estimated seventeen million workers are *"actively disengaged."* That is 15 percent of the U.S. workforce who report that they are not only unhappy, but are actively undermining the efforts of their co-workers![31] Do the math—almost three out of every four employees are disconnected, disengaged, and disinterested in the company's objectives. Can you imagine what impact this is having on productivity?

Employee Motivation

Feeling completely lost in the tide of employee discontent, and not knowing exactly how to solve the problem, some managers consider how they might "motivate" their employees. There is this persistent idea that great coaches, great managers, and charismatic leaders are able to motivate those that work or play on their teams with heart-tugging orations and emotional speeches that create victory against all odds: the proverbial "Win-one-for-the-Gipper" approach.

George Gipp, Notre Dame's first football All-American, provided the source material for sports' most famous speech in 1920. One of the era's greatest all-around players, Gipp went to Notre Dame to play baseball, but was recruited by the legendary Knute Rockne to play football. A potent force on offense and defense, Gipp also returned kicks and punts. In the final two years of his career, the Fighting Irish never lost, finishing 19-0-1 and outscoring opponents 560-27.[32] Sadly, Gipp succumbed to pneumonia and infection on December 14, 1920, two weeks after his selection as an All-American.

The story is told that Rockne visited Gipp in the hospital as he lay near death, and agreed to honor his final deathbed request:

1-on-1 Management

"I've got to go, Rock. It's all right. I'm not afraid. Sometime, Rock, when the team is up against it, when things are wrong and the breaks are beating the boys—tell them to go in there with all they've got and win just one for the Gipper. I don't know where I'll be then, Rock. But I'll know about it, and I'll be happy."[33]

The stuff of legends (and Ronald Reagan movies).

Several years later, in 1928, Rockne seized the opportunity to use Gipp's inspirational words. Rockne was enduring his worst season as the head coach at Notre Dame. In thirteen years as the head coach of the Fighting Irish, Rockne's squad would leave the field as the losing team only 12 times, but 4 of those losses would come in 1928.

As the end of the season neared, Notre Dame's record stood at 4-2 with three very difficult opponents remaining on the schedule: Army, Carnegie Tech, and USC. Injuries had decimated the squad and the chance for the unthinkable, a losing season, was a very real possibility. Entering the game against undefeated arch-rival Army, Rockne thought the time had come to honor the fabled last request of the Gipper.

The teams had battled to a scoreless tie at halftime, and in the quiet of the locker room, Rockne recounted the heroics of Gipp's career at Notre Dame. The school's first All-American. Perhaps the greatest player ever in the fabled history of Notre Dame football. A man who had given everything he had to the team, but had been struck down early, in the prime of his life. Rockne ended his moving story by sharing Gipp's final deathbed request. "George Gipp asked me to wait until the situation

Introduction to 1-on-1 Management™

seemed hopeless, then ask a Notre Dame team to go out and beat Army for him," he told them. "This is the day, boys, and you are the team."[34]

The impact was dramatic. Moved to tears, and with fierce resolve, the team stormed back onto the field at Yankee Stadium, prepared to do anything necessary to wrench victory away from the Cadets. The Irish snapped a 6-6 tie on a 32-yard TD pass late in the fourth quarter, but the game was very much in doubt following a 55-yard kick-off return by Army. The Cadets marched all the way to the 4-yard line with only seconds to play, but time expired as Army was stopped just short of the goal line on the game's final play. The bitter struggle ended in a 12-6 victory for the Irish—a momentous win for the Gipper![35]

Funny thing about those Knute Rockne speeches. There are some rather significant prerequisites for them to be successful: the team has to believe in you as their leader, they must be completely committed to the task at hand, and it always helps to have a fair level of talent in order to compete. Rockne's Fighting Irish football teams? They produced 105 wins in thirteen years. Six national championships. Five undefeated seasons. His .881 winning percentage is still an NCAA record.[36] The Irish had great players, and in Rockne, perhaps the greatest innovator and coach of his day. His players loved him.

Rockne's speech makes for a phenomenal story, but unfortunately, speeches alone don't create player commitment. It would be a lot easier if they did, I suppose, but the road to organizational success is paved with trust, and trust isn't earned with speeches. Teams play well together when they believe in each other, when they believe in their mission, and when they believe in their leader.

1-on-1 Management

Positive leadership actions influence team members over a course of time, developing a belief and a trust in the leader. As this trust matures and is consistently reinforced, commitment to the task at hand follows. Employees become "engaged" and interested in driving the objectives of the company, utilizing their talents and abilities to make positive contributions to a well-defined mission. It is this environment that allows motivated employees to flourish. It is within this environment that great managers can elicit performance that team members had not considered possible. Employees can be roused to do more than they themselves believe they are capable of doing. This is what Knute Rockne was able to do, and this is real leadership.

Great managers understand this.

One-on-One Management in Action

Great managers recognize that the foundations of trust have to be constructed before the walls of commitment can be raised. Employees won't run through brick walls for a paycheck. They will, however, plow through any number of obstacles for a manager that believes in them, recognizes their contribution, develops their potential, and creates opportunities to be a part of something special. Great managers understand that the primary motivation they provide for employees is to put them in the right environment to capitalize on their capabilities.

What is it exactly that great managers know that you don't? First, they know that their primary responsibility is to develop the potential of people. More importantly, they know *how* to develop people. They recognize that managing is about leading, and leading is contingent on developing trust; that trust precedes

Introduction to 1-on-1 Management™

commitment and commitment is necessary for extraordinary performance. At the same time, the most critical understanding that great managers have is that effective management requires individual attention.

> **1-on-1 Principle™:** Developing employee performance and capability is a one-on-one process.

Elzbieta Górska-Kolodziejczyk works for International Paper in Kwidzyn, Poland. Formerly a state-owned facility in communist Poland, it is now a private corporation with over 1,600 employees. The only female middle-manager in the facility, Górska was asked to assume the manager's position for the company's warehouse operation, a department with 24 employees—mostly men. Her remarkable story is recounted in detail in the *Gallup Management Journal* in a story entitled "A Manager's Revolutionary Idea at International Paper."

Her *revolutionary* idea? To recognize and encourage her employees, an idea she decided could be done most effectively by meeting with them individually:

> To help her better manage the team, Górska began *meeting individually* [italics mine] with her workers. "I started with listening to them, what they have to say, how they see it, how they would want the work to be organized, what more would they expect, what kind of work materials are they lacking," she says. "At the same time, I wrote down their problems and issues they wanted to be resolved. When we met again, I reported on what had been done. It also brought us closer."[37]

1-on-1 Management

Górska faced a number of obstacles in her two-year quest to change the work environment of the warehouse. First, Polish culture doesn't respond to praise and recognition in the same way that Americans do; employees were suspicious of her motives, particularly the men. Second, there were a number of significant issues to overcome in the operations of the warehouse, including a poor system of organization and the lack of a computer system. Third, morale had plummeted in the past as warehouse employees felt overlooked and neglected by the company.

Despite the hurdles and the skepticism of her employees, Górska's patience and determination paid off. Her approach to management produced huge dividends for the company, driving employee engagement numbers from the worst quartile to the top, while top brass commended her for the impressive improvements in operational efficiency.

1-on-1 Management™

Górska's story is positive proof that many barriers can be overcome when managers commit themselves to the process of developing employees rather than simply directing their efforts. Her efforts at International Paper illustrate some of the key components of 1-on-1 Management™:

- Creating an environment of engagement through encouragement and recognition

- Meeting individually with employees (see 1-on-1 Meetings™ - Chapter 10)

- Focusing on effective communication, consistent feedback, and one-on-one dialogue

Introduction to 1-on-1 Management™

Each of these elements contributes to creating a professional and productive relationship with an employee, one that is based on trust. As the relationship develops, a mutual understanding ensues; understanding is nurtured through the use of feedback and dialogue. The 1-on-1 Meeting™ is the backbone of this process. Whereas the typical review process is a once-a-year event, the 1-on-1 Meeting™ provides a vehicle to 1) meet on a consistent basis (usually each week), 2) communicate expectations, 3) give and receive feedback, 4) assess and revise performance on a consistent basis, and 5) coach the employee to develop their talents and skills.

It is so much easier to review last week's activities and make necessary adjustments than it is to review an entire year's worth of activity. The truth is that only a few things really stand out in a manager's mind from the previous twelve months, and there is a tendency to evaluate personnel based on their performance during the last several weeks.

The emphasis on communication is absolutely vital to organizational health. In chapter 3, we learned that employees clearly need to be "in on things," and it is not difficult to understand that people are more productive and effective when they understand what they are working towards and how their work contributes to the overall objectives of the company. VSP Capital General Partner John Hamm describes the consequences of communication failure in a *Harvard Business Review* article:

> In the absence of clear communication that satisfies the urgent desire to know what the boss is really thinking, people imagine all kinds of motives. The result is often sloppy behavior and misalignment that can cost a company dearly.[38]

1-on-1 Management

Of course, communication takes on various forms—policy and procedure, corporate information, praise and recognition, performance review, casting a vision, and much more. As we will see in chapter 9, encouragement and recognition are vital components to creating a workplace environment that engages employees. In *The Carrot Principle*, authors Adrian Gostick and Chester Elton were able to quantify the results of recognition through extensive employee surveys. The results? Companies that use recognition effectively outperform those that fail to recognize employees adequately.[39]

Authors Tom Rath and Don Clifton discuss the importance of recognition and praise in the best-seller *How Full is Your Bucket*? Drawing on the results of a Gallup survey of four million workers on the topics of recognition and praise, they discovered that the number one reason people leave their jobs is because they don't feel appreciated. In fact, 65 percent of those surveyed indicated they had received no workplace recognition at all in the previous year. On the other hand, those that were regularly recognized and praised had higher productivity, better safety records, and were likely to stay with the organization longer.[40]

Other vital aspects of communication include the process of creating and fulfilling expectations. Managers have expectations of their employees' work performance, attitude, dependability, and many other items. Conversely, employees have expectations of their managers—to provide direction, to help when necessary, to create opportunities, and so on. We will look at expectations in depth, from both sides, in chapters 6 through 8.

The final component of 1-on-1 Management™ is employee career and skills development through coaching and mentoring (chapter 11). In conjunction with the 1-on-1 Development Plan™ (chapter 12), a manager is able to identify employee strengths and weaknesses, review past performance, and create a well-defined plan for developing skills and advancing their careers. An effective development plan allows an employee to run the race with a finish line in sight; it creates an underlying purpose and a reason to excel.

Conclusion

1-on-1 Management™ principles are not revolutionary, but neither are they theoretical. They are a compilation of management concepts that great managers use to produce real and lasting results. A word of warning, however—workplace cultures are not transformed overnight. Like anything that introduces change into the workplace, there will likely be some initial push-back from a few employees; some may express skepticism or anxiety about meeting with you one-on-one, assuming the worst about your motives. It will be critically important for you to communicate early and often regarding your objectives, and to be consistent with your words and your actions.

The good news is that skepticism will give way to enthusiasm—at least for your talented team members. Employees generally will welcome the opportunity to gain an audience with the boss, and the results of individual attention will begin to show very quickly. As you begin the 1-on-1 Management™ process, the primary objective will be to open the lines of communication and reinforce the idea that you are interested in learning about the individual interests of each employee.

1-on-1 Insights™

- Remember, employees *join* companies, but they *quit* managers.

- Managers motivate employees by creating a work atmosphere that produces trust, rewards performance, and focuses on people.

- Great managers see people as their priority, so they work to develop leadership skills (leadership is influence, remember?).

- Employees are human beings; they want to be recognized, praised, and valued.

- Managers almost always get in return what they first give to their employees.

- 1-on-1 Management™ creates the ability to build trust, communicate effectively, review performance and provide feedback, and deal with challenges directly.

Effective Communication in the Workplace

The culture of an organization is widely determined by the quality of its communication

"Open communication requires no dollar outlay, yet it is the best investment you can make when trying to align your company around results. And honest, two-way communication includes a heavy proportion of listening."

—Roger Connors and Tom Smith,
Journey to the Emerald City

On January 16, 2003, the space shuttle *Columbia* thundered off Launch Pad 39A at the Kennedy Space Center, embarking on its 28th mission into space. STS-107, the 113th overall flight of the Space Transport System, was slated as a 16-day earth science research mission and staffed with a crew of seven: Commander Rick Husband, Pilot William McCool, Payload Commander Michael Anderson, Payload Specialist Ilan Ramon (the first Israeli astronaut), Mission Specialist Kalpana Chawla, Mission Specialist David Brown, and Mission Specialist Laurel Clark.

On the morning of the mission's final day, *Columbia* was 175 miles above the Indian Ocean—flying upside-down and backward at a speed of almost 5 miles per second. At 8:15

a.m. EST, the shuttle executed a de-orbit burn that rolled the spacecraft over into the traditional flying position (forward and right-side-up), and marked the beginning of its return to earth.

At 8:44 a.m., *Columbia* was streaking over the Pacific Ocean as it began to enter the earth's discernible atmosphere at an altitude of 400,000 feet. During the first 6 minutes of re-entry, temperatures on the leading edge of the shuttle's wings would catapult to 2,500 degrees Fahrenheit and reach nearly 3,000 degrees at its peak.

At 8:53 a.m., *Columbia* had dropped to an altitude of 230,000 feet and was crossing the California coast, just over 20 minutes away from its scheduled landing time of 9:16 a.m. In the next few minutes, witnesses would observe several bright flashes of light around the shuttle, and Mission Control would note pressure changes in the two tires on the craft's left landing gear. At 8:59 a.m., Rick Husband's final radio transmission was cut off in mid-sentence.

Perhaps you can remember where you were on that fateful Saturday morning. Television footage revealed the worst. Thirty-nine miles above the earth, traveling at a speed of 12,500 miles per hour, the unthinkable happened—the Space Shuttle *Columbia* simply disintegrated, spewing debris over hundreds of square miles.

Subsequent investigation discovered that the cause of the catastrophic accident was created only eighty-one seconds into Columbia's flight. A piece of foam insulation about the size of a brief case, dislodged during lift-off, struck and damaged the leading edge of Columbia's left wing. The resultant defect in the craft's thermal protection system allowed "superheated air to penetrate the leading-edge insulation and progressively melt the aluminum structure of the left wing, resulting in a weakening of the structure until increasing aerodynamic forces caused loss of control, failure of the wing, and breakup of the Orbiter."[41]

At the same time, other significant concerns surfaced during the investigation. Although the mechanical failure that created the *Columbia* disaster was identified and well-documented, systemic issues were also revealed to have played a critical role in the tragedy:

> Cultural traits and organizational practices detrimental to safety were allowed to develop, including: reliance on past success as a substitute for sound engineering practices (such as testing to understand why systems were not performing in accordance with requirements/specifications); organizational barriers that prevented effective communication of critical safety information and stifled professional differences of opinion . . .[42]

Organizational barriers negatively impacted safety, and ultimately, it was *poor communication* that created the circumstances leading to the loss of *Columbia* and its seven crew members:

> The Board believes that *deficiencies in communication . . . were a foundation for the Columbia accident* [italics mine]. These deficiencies are byproducts of a cumbersome, bureaucratic, and highly complex Shuttle Program structure and the absence of authority in two key program areas that

are responsible for integrating information across all programs and elements in the Shuttle program.[43]

Regrettably, NASA seems not to have learned from its past mistakes. A complete reading of the 248-page *Columbia Accident Investigation Board* report makes it clear that organizational problems that contributed to the loss of the *Columbia* were also instrumental in the tragic loss of the space shuttle *Challenger* on January 28, 1986:

> The echoes did not stop there. The foam debris hit was not the single cause of the *Columbia* accident, just as the failure of the joint seal that permitted O-ring erosion was not the single cause of *Challenger*. Both *Columbia* and *Challenger* were lost also because of the failure of NASA's organizational system.[44]

Due to the strategic value of its mission, NASA must persevere through this second catastrophic failure. One can only hope that deficiencies in communication and organizational barriers will not create a third failure of this magnitude.

The Critical Role of Communication in the Workplace

The average manager does not typically deal with life-and-death issues in the workplace, nor do most businesses have the size or complexity of NASA. Still, the *Columbia* tragedy vividly illustrates the critical role that communication plays in the health of any organization. Rather than the loss of life, "catastrophe" in the average business usually means financial loss—the loss of a customer, the loss of a valued employee, or the loss of opportunity.

1-on-1 Principle™: Poor communication creates the majority of workplace issues.

It is important, first of all, to define "communication." Managers tend to see communication as telling employees what to do. In some cases, they might even confirm that the employee understands completely. But communication is much more than just issuing marching orders. The many facets of communication include encouragement, recognition, instruction, directives, feedback, clarification, identification of objectives, and much more. More importantly, as I will emphasize in chapter 7, every word and action of a manager is observed and interpreted by each employee. Your actions, your words, and your decisions are constantly monitored and compared to each other, and these daily actions directly influence the judgments that are formed regarding your character and your competence.

1-on-1 Principle™: Communication is much more than words; it includes your actions, the way you do things, and the things you *don't* do.

As we learned in chapter 3, two significant aspects of communication—and two things that employees need to remain effectively engaged in the workplace—are full appreciation for work done and a sense of being "in" on things. However, there are several factors that negatively impact these, and all other, facets of the communication process: the choice of communication media, insufficient training in communication skills, a corporate culture that inhibits communication (the *Columbia* disaster is a good example), and a multitude of barriers that limit or prevent good communication.

Regarding Communication Media

The medium used to communicate is often quite critical. For example, a recent *Time* magazine article revealed that *poor handwriting* results in over 7,000 deaths annually:

> Doctors' sloppy handwriting kills more than 7,000 people annually. It's a shocking statistic, and, according to a July 2006 report from the National Academies of Science's Institute of Medicine (IOM), preventable medication mistakes also injure more than 1.5 million Americans annually. Many such errors result from unclear abbreviations and dosage indications and illegible writing on some of the 3.2 billion prescriptions written in the U.S. every year.[45]

This revelation is staggering. A physician's inability to write legible instructions causes an average of over nineteen deaths every single day! The proposed solution to this problem? Simply change the communication *medium*; transition the doctor to an electronic system of writing prescriptions and orders.

In another common situation, a manager will often rely on e-mail messages or voice mail for critical communications.

Effective Communication in the Workplace

Fearful of a face-to-face confrontation, the manager will opt to communicate impersonally, although research indicates that only 7 percent of meaning is communicated by the words themselves when discerning feelings and attitudes. The balance—and vast majority—of meaning is derived from tonality (38 percent) and non-verbal content (55 percent).[46]

With only words on a screen to work with, the recipient will rarely put the message into any emotional context other than the one they already understand; in other words, it is incredibly difficult to influence people or change their minds on an emotional issue by e-mail! Losing the majority of intended meaning—from the body language and tonality that would normally accompany a message—only leads to further confusion and increasing resentment which, left unchecked, will eventually create more significant issues for the manager. How many times have you seen a tenuous situation spiral out of control because two parties refuse to sit down face-to-face and discuss the issues—choosing instead to fire at each other through e-mail?

One of the primary reasons that 1-on-1 Management™ is so effective is that it relies heavily on face-to-face communication, whereas traditional managers have come to rely mostly on electronic media—e-mail, voice mail, text messages, and so forth. Further, even when messages are conveyed verbally, it is in meetings—often with large numbers of participants. People are frequently uncomfortable speaking up in front of their peers for fear of asking a silly question or saying something wrong, and effective workplace communication requires dialogue, not monologue.

1-on-1 Management

Regarding Barriers to Communication

Even when conditions are optimal—that is, adequate training is provided that produces skilled communicators, the corporate culture encourages frank communication, and managers learn when and how to properly utilize the most effective communication medium—there are still a number of "barriers" that will prevent effective communication. Barriers are issues or circumstances that prevent the successful transfer of information: a difference in the understanding of language, differences in perceptions (created by different cultures, backgrounds, experiences, etc.), different or competing agendas, or anything that creates a mental distraction while trying to communicate (personal issues are a prime example).

A frightening example of communication barriers occurred during the 1992 Los Angeles riots. When south-central Los Angeles erupted following the Rodney King verdict, more than 2,300 people were injured and over 50 people were killed. At least 12,000 arrests were made and property damages exceeded $1 billion, impacting 3,100 businesses.[47]

During this chaos, police officers responded to a domestic dispute call, accompanied by a number of Marines to provide back-up. As the officers approached the door of the house, they were greeted with two shotgun rounds that were fired through the door and struck the officers. One of the officers turned and yelled to the Marines: "Cover me!" Acknowledging the request, the Marines fired over two hundred rounds into the house.[48]

This was a miscommunication of potentially fatal proportions. For a trained police officer, the phrase "Cover me!" means to point your weapon and prepare to respond, if necessary. This is what the officer intended to communicate in this situation. However, in the military, the same phrase means to lay down a heavy suppressing fire in order to provide cover while someone maneuvers into a new position. While no one was injured in this incident, the potential for catastrophe was enormous as a number of children were later found in the house. In this case, the barrier to effective communication was the lack of a common understanding of language.

Perhaps the most common barrier to effective face-to-face communication is what is referred to as "noise." This can be actual noise—like trying to have a conversation in a crowded restaurant—but there are many other sources of noise. Noise simply refers to distractions that prevent a communicator from focusing on the conversation at hand.

A frequent culprit is the personal issues that arise—a sick child, overdue bills, the death of a parent, problems at school, marital difficulties, and so on. While engaged in a conversation, these issues can distract from one's ability to listen because the mind is elsewhere. During communication training, I always ask participants if personal issues affect work performance. The answer is always "yes." Always. And while it is true for an employee, it is also true for a manager.

Other types of noise that may adversely affect communication include things like deadlines, stress, worry, fear, fatigue, lack of interest, or even selfish motivations. Anything that prevents an individual from focusing on the message and the person delivering the message is "noise" that prevents, or diminishes, understanding.

Communicating Through Change

In today's business environment, change has become the norm rather than the exception—companies grow or merge, new technologies are introduced, objectives change, strategies evolve, and leadership changes. Companies are constantly in a state of flux, and each transition can create anxiety, discomfort, or even fear.

This means that one of the critical areas of communication for any leader is the ability to communicate effectively during times of change. Harvard Business School professor John Kotter, widely considered one of the premier authorities on leadership and change management, describes the critical nature of communication during times of change:

> Transformation is impossible unless hundreds or thousands of people are willing to help, often to the point of making short-term sacrifices. Employees will not make sacrifices, even if they are unhappy with the status quo, unless they believe that useful change is possible. Without credible communication, and a lot of it, the hearts and minds of the troops are never captured.[49]

Managers are often stunned to discover that they fare quite poorly in communicating during times of change, despite numerous memos and group meetings. I have certainly been one of those people! While communicating was always a priority for me as a manager, I was often disappointed to learn that some employees felt I had not communicated adequately, despite what I considered to be great effort in doing so.

Kotter provides a critical insight to this problem when he states that communication must be credible. "Credible" implies that the challenge for any manager is to understand that communication is far more than information delivery. Managers must communicate the "why" of change as well as the who, what, when, and where. Further, because change impacts each individual differently, mass communication is often lacking in the details that allow each employee to resolve personal issues.

Questions and Answers

The question, then, is what should you do to communicate more effectively? The answer, I think, is pretty simple, but the devil, as they say, is in the details:

Ask effective questions and listen carefully to the answers.

In fact, looking back at what employees really want (from chapter 3), we find that only appreciation communicates value more effectively than "being in on things." "Being in on things" means that the manager tells employees why things are happening and solicits their input and ideas about how to deal with those issues.

Questions and answers. For the average manager, this should be eye-opening. After all, most managers see themselves as the person that should be *answering* questions rather than asking them. You know the drill: issue directives, field questions, repeat.

When Michael Abrashoff assumed command of the USS *Benfold* in June 1997, he realized that the traditional command-

1-on-1 Management

and-control approach was not working. His evidence? All 310 sailors aboard *Benfold* cheered enthusiastically as the previous commander left the ship during the change-of-command ceremony. In addition, Abrashoff was well aware that only 46 percent of sailors on average remain in the navy past the second tour of duty, a fact that not only compromises combat effectiveness, but also costs the navy an enormous amount of money. Costs to recruit and train a sailor to serve on the $1 billion warship exceed $100,000.[50]

> It began, as I said, that first day aboard the *Benfold*, as my crew derisively cheered their departing commander. Clearly, his approach to leadership had failed. It was, sadly, an approach that I knew all too well. Command and control to the max. Do exactly what I say, when I say it, no questions, no comments.[51]

Abrashoff realized that altering this environment would require, first and foremost, a significant change in his perspective as a leader. After taking command of the *Benfold*, he made the decision to meet with each sailor individually to ask questions about their personal and career goals. During these meetings, his objective was to treat the crew member as the most important person on the ship at that moment, and to ask them what they would change on the ship, given the opportunity:

> Getting them to contribute in a meaningful way to each life-or-death mission isn't just a matter of training and discipline. It's a matter of knowing who they are and where

they're coming from—and linking that knowledge to our purpose.

Within two days of when new crew members arrive, I sit down with them face-to-face. I try to learn something about each of them: Why did they join the navy? What's their family situation like? What are their goals while they're in the navy—and beyond? How can I help them chart a course through life? Ultimately, I consider it my job to improve my little 300-person piece of society. And that's as much a part of the bottom line as operational readiness is.[52]

The results of Abrashoff's leadership change were nothing short of extraordinary. In 1998, the *Benfold* completed the navy's pre-deployment training cycle in record time, and was awarded the Spokane Trophy for achieving the best combat readiness in the fleet. Sailor retention on the ship skyrocketed to 100 percent, saving the navy millions of dollars in recruiting and training costs. In addition, the changes suggested by the sailors on the ship saved the navy an additional $1.4 million in 1998 alone.[53]

Abrashoff's story demonstrates two significant principles. First, he met with each sailor face-to-face; that is to say, one-on-one. Second, he asked several good questions. Great managers understand that effective communication is done directly, and, most importantly, includes a significant measure of listening.

1-on-1 Management

The Art of Listening

If asking the right questions is critical, then listening carefully to the answers is the proverbial pot of gold at the end of the rainbow. While many managers consider good communication to be defined by how well they lecture, run meetings, and issue memos, communication is actually an *exchange* of information. In other words, good workplace communication means that a manager must create a dialogue. However, as the old saying goes, *"two monologues do not create a dialogue!"*

It seems abundantly clear that managers as a group are very poor listeners. The first challenge a manager encounters is that he or she typically has several, if not dozens, of tasks and projects under their supervision, and multi-tasking is perhaps the greatest enemy of effective listening. Second, listening is a skill, one that must be developed and consistently practiced, but is rarely taught and almost never assessed as a qualification for management. Third, misunderstanding what effective management really is leads many to believe that solving problems and issuing orders, rather than communicating effectively, are the manager's most important objectives.

The foundation of listening effectively is encapsulated in the words of Stephen Covey, author of *The 7 Habits of Highly Effective People*. He asserts that one of those seven habits is to "seek first to understand"[54]—arguably, the polar opposite of what most managers, indeed, most people in general, regularly practice. Clearly, the objective of listening is to understand the other person. Many, however, would assert that a manager's first objective is to "seek first to *be understood,*" that is, to have the employee understand them. After all, a good manager must ensure that employees understand what is expected of them, understand how to do their jobs correctly, and understand the objectives of their current assignments.

These things are all true in context. However, with regard to developing people and building trust with employees, effective communication is essential. Further, effective communication in this context is mostly about listening *and* seeking to understand. Unfortunately, as M. Scott Peck observes, we are frequently guilty of having little or no interest in understanding the other person's point-of-view:

> Even though we may feel that we are listening very hard, what we are usually doing is listening selectively, with a present agenda in mind, wondering as we listen how we can achieve certain desired results and get the conversation over with as quickly as possible, or redirect it in ways more satisfactory to us.[55]

Thankfully, listening is a skill that can be learned and developed. The key to being a good listener is to start with Covey's admonition—seek *first* to listen to (understand) the person with whom you are speaking. Resist the urge to quick-fix a problem, and don't assume that you know what the problem is. Instead, ask further questions to clarify meaning.

Undoubtedly, asking good questions and listening carefully to the answers is much more difficult than issuing a memo, sending a text message, or simply telling an employee what to do. However, effective communication is the cornerstone of great management, and effective communication is dependent on questions and answers.

Five Areas to PROVE Yourself an Effective Communicator

As we have seen, effective communication is not limited to one or two areas. It encompasses a myriad of workplace situations. My experience has taught me that there are five key areas in which effective managers learn to communicate effectively:

- **P**ersonal communication: Learning the goals and ambitions of each employee is necessary in establishing rapport, and ultimately trust, with those you manage. By learning about the things that are important to each employee, *you create vital connections* between the employee and the company. At the same time, learn from Commander Abrashoff's example—ask each of your employees what changes they would make in their work given the opportunity.

- **R**ecognition: Recognizing, encouraging, and rewarding work performance is critical to developing a high-performance workplace (we will explore recognition in-depth in chapter 9). By recognizing and encouraging excellence, *you create value in your employees*.

- **O**bjectives: Providing clear instructions regarding the results you desire is necessary to provide focus for your organization. Without a definitive target to shoot at, even the world's best marksman cannot hit the bull's-eye. At the same time, by supplying the opportunity to use their talents to achieve specific objectives and accomplish critical tasks, *you create confidence in your employees' own competence* and help them derive satisfaction from their work.

- **V**ision: Constructing a verbal picture of the company and its direction (Who are we? What do we do? Where are we going? What do we stand for?) is an important part of building team unity. Additionally, one of the hallmarks of a great leader is the ability to help individuals believe they can be more, and accomplish more, than they believe they can—that they can achieve great things or reach meaningful objectives. By providing a clear picture of the team's mission, *you create purpose* within your team.

- **E**xpectations: Establishing the standards for performance excellence on your team and ensuring that each employee understands their individual contribution to the company's objectives improves performance management. Many managers dread performance reviews, believing them to be too subjective. However, by communicating your objectives and expectations clearly, *you create a culture of accountability* and turn the performance review process into a positive exercise.

Conclusion

I have an uncle who is a remarkable guitar player. Anyone who has heard him play readily agrees that he can "play the frets off a guitar." He has been playing for a very long time, starting as a teenager and continuing off-and-on for over thirty years. The thing is, if you ask him about his ability, he will tell you that he considers himself to be a pretty average player at best. He has told me several times over the years that the better he gets, the more he understands just how much more there is to learn.

1-on-1 Management

I used to just shake my head and laugh at his modesty; then I started playing guitar myself. After many years of learning to play, I now understand. As I slowly improve, I am continually aware of how much more there is to learn.

Communication, especially the critically important skill of listening, is like that. Managers who communicate well always seem to feel that there is considerable room for improvement, which leads them to work harder and harder to be more effective.

As you begin to implement the 1-on-1 Management™ ideas and techniques, you should place a heavy premium on communication—*real* communication.

Clarify until you understand. Refuse to make assumptions; ask more questions. Solicit feedback and encourage employee input. Invariably, improvements in employee communication will lead directly to proportional improvements in employee performance.

1-on-1 Insights™

- Poor communication destroys corporate cultures. The first objective of any manager should be to open lines of communication with employees.

- Everything a manager does is communication: the actions you take, the actions you *don't* take, how you react, the comments you make, the words you say, the way you listen. All of these things—and more—are constantly scrutinized by employees and scrubbed for meaning.

- Nobody knows better than the employees what things should be changed or improved in the company. Why not ask them?

- Communication is not defined as a monologue. It takes two people to communicate effectively—and a healthy dose of listening will greatly improve your understanding.

The Power of Expectations

If expectations are not clearly communicated, conflict is the inevitable result

"Great communicators have an appreciation for positioning. They understand the people they're trying to reach and what they can and can't hear. They send their message in through an open door rather than trying to push it through a wall."

—John P. Kotter

In 1983, I interviewed for a position at an office furniture store looking for a "talented and energetic" person to eventually become the manager of a second retail location. The owner of the store liked my athletic background and my competitive nature, and judged me to be just what he was looking for. At twenty-three years of age, I was young and hungry, willing to work hard and do whatever was necessary to be successful, so I enthusiastically accepted the offer to be a "management trainee."

My first day on the job should have warned me that things were going to end badly. Arriving the first day, like any other typical new hire, I was excited to meet the other employees and find out how I would begin in my new position. I was anxious to get a handle on the time frame for working into the management role, and curious to see how the training process was designed.

Instead, I was hurriedly introduced to a couple of front office employees as the "new guy," shuffled off to the office supply side of the store, and handed a retail catalog to learn about staplers and paper clips. At least, that is what I thought I was doing. Later, I realized it was only something to keep me busy since they didn't really have anything prepared—no training, no orientation, nothing.

Eventually, it became clear that the immediate position the company wanted me to fill was as a retail salesperson and the management position was contingent on success in that role. My job was to greet prospective customers, immediately identify their office furniture needs, and then close a substantial sale before the customer left the building—sales skills I didn't come close to having. Additionally, the company provided very little training on the products we were selling, and I had little understanding of the industry, our competitors, available financing options, and other critical details necessary to close large deals in a single presentation.

My boss was a great guy to hang around with—enthusiastic, intelligent, and a constant source of laughs—but he rarely communicated with employees on a personal level. As is often the case with multi-tasking managers, he was much too busy working to develop the people that worked for him. Consequently, I quickly became frustrated at the lack of direction, and you certainly didn't need a crystal ball to realize that that I was beginning to be perceived as a problem. I wasn't setting the world on fire as a "manager trainee" or as an inside salesperson.

The Power of Expectations

When the boss fired me, he offered these words of wisdom: "Stay out of sales. You'll never make it. Get into operations or something else."

The whole episode served as a constant motivation in my career. Just a few years later, I would be recognized as the national Salesperson of the Year for the medical company I worked for—twice.

My personal experience was created by a number of circumstances, but the bottom line was that I simply didn't get the job I expected and the company didn't get the results they expected. It reminds me of an old joke about marriages that go awry:

> *The honeymoon is over when she starts wondering what happened to the man she married, and he starts wondering what happened to the girl he didn't.*

She wonders why he changed. He wonders why she didn't. Or vice versa. The common denominator in either of these situations, marriage or workplace, is expectations. More accurately, perhaps, it is the lack of alignment of those expectations.

Marriage counselors often discover that troubled marriages are characterized by partners who feign interest in things their prospective mates enjoy that they never really intend to do after they get married. For men, it might include things like Meg Ryan movies, long walks in the park, opening her door; you know, the stuff most guys might not ever do until they date the woman of their dreams. For women it might be things like Arnold Schwarzenegger movies, watching football all day Saturday, working on the car together . . . you get the picture.

However, by doing those things while dating, men and women establish expectations; they expect that all of those considerate and unselfish acts will continue right into marriage! In some cases, they do. In others, not so much.

The exact same dynamics are at work in the workplace. When you interview a potential candidate for a position, that individual presents the very best of their education, work history, and skills. They recount vividly their successes in previous jobs and provide glowing references. You are regaled with numerous examples of how they solved problems, demonstrated initiative, and dealt with workplace issues. Weaknesses? Please.

At the same time, employers describe, without question, the best place in the world to go to work. Great people. Great benefits. Everything any employee could ask for, including a desperate need for the candidate's talent and abilities—who, by the way, is characterized in glowing terms as "exactly the right person for the job." The proverbial "match made in heaven."

How long this "honeymoon" lasts is largely a function of the reception and introduction an employee receives the first few weeks on the job. Again, great managers know that employees join organizations but quit managers. How well the manager establishes and aligns expectations, initially and long-term, will determine in large part how the employee ultimately performs.

1-on-1 Principle™: To maximize work performance and ensure job satisfaction, the expectations of the manager and employee must be mutually understood.

Employees arrive on the first day of employment with a set of expectations established during the hiring process through

The Power of Expectations

observation and conversation. They have great confidence in their abilities, have little doubt that they can and will excel given the opportunity, and expect to make a positive contribution to the company's performance. They also believe that the company needs their skills and is ready to support and encourage the application of those talents.

If detailed workplace expectations are not established from the very beginning of employment, it is like driving without a destination—everything is working, but the employee may very well be going in the wrong direction. Perhaps Yogi Berra said it best: "You got to be careful if you don't know where you're going, because you might not get there."[56]

Conflict is Inevitable

Aligned expectations are established by clear communication and reinforced by actions that are consistent with that communication. Problems that arise as a result of misaligned expectations are often attributed to a "personality conflict," or the employee is characterized as someone who "just doesn't get it." While there may be some truth to each of these observations in certain circumstances, it is just as likely that the company or manager has communicated poorly.

In the United States Army, there are four major reasons given for human error, or performance failure:

1. Standards are unclear, impractical, or nonexistent.
2. Standards exist, but are unknown.
3. Standards are known, but not enforced.
4. Standards are known, but not followed.[57]

1-on-1 Management

The army has the expectation that a soldier in any position will execute assigned duties safely and properly. Whether it is firing a weapon, repairing a vehicle, or working in administrative support, the army expects that standards will be clear, known by the troops, and enforced by leadership. If standards exist, but are unknown (No. 2), it is characterized as a "training failure." If the standards are known, but not enforced (No. 3), it is known to be a "leadership failure." Army officers strive to provide strong leadership by ensuring that adequate training is provided and all standards are consistently enforced.

Therefore, while the army expects that a soldier will make mistakes, they never want those mistakes to fall into any category except the last one. Once standards (expectations) are established, known, and enforced, all performance can be evaluated and attributed directly to the soldier. Adjustments can be made as necessary, and performance should be improved as a result. However, if expectations (standards) have not been established, errors that occur are difficult to evaluate and correct.

This principle is just as true in the workplace. There are many expectations—or standards—that should be clearly communicated to an employee: workplace culture, levels of authority, job requirement, quality standards, safety standards, opportunity for advancement, and perhaps the most important, performance standards.

Aligning Expectations

Savvy leaders understand that people will rise to the level of established expectations, even, in many cases, when those expectations are greater than the ability the individual may perceive that they possess.

In the world of education, a significant percentage of the worst-performing schools, based on academic indices, are high-poverty schools. In 2005, a Kentucky study published findings that sought to answer the question of why certain high-poverty schools were dramatic exceptions to this rule. Using criteria established by an audit committee, eight schools were identified in the state that were categorized as high-poverty, high-performing schools. The eight schools are a mix of urban and rural institutions, ranging in enrollment from 168 to 653 students, and exhibit a population of minority students ranging from less than 1 percent to 70 percent.[58]

Why did these schools succeed where other high-poverty schools did not? The answer is not technology, planning processes, or even support from the school district. The study was able to identify a number of commonalities in these high-poverty, high-performing schools, but perhaps the most significant was the expectations that teacher and staff had for their students:

> High expectations . . . were communicated in concrete ways. Principals held high expectations for faculty and staff, who held high expectations for themselves and the students. There was a strong belief that all students could succeed academically and that faculty and staff were capable of making this happen.[59]

Specifically, the study discovered that "(school) leadership creates experiences to foster belief that all can learn at high levels," and that "teachers accept their professional role in student success and failure."[60]

1-on-1 Management

Imagine this: teachers who believe in a student's ability to succeed, expect them to succeed, and accept their role and responsibility in making that success a reality! Of course, the success demonstrated in these schools is much more than just an intellectual belief in success. Administrators and teachers work diligently and tirelessly to ensure that the students perform as well as their middle-to-upper income counterparts. The mission of the school is to provide the means and opportunity for the students to succeed, and this mission is clearly communicated to everyone involved:

> The entire school community appeared to be on the same page with regard to what was being taught, what performance expectations were, and where each teacher's focus fit into the broader curriculum of the school. Teaching was part of a larger collaborative effort, not a solitary activity involving individuals who decided on their own what to teach and when to teach it.[61]

Question: Won't the same principles apply in the workplace? From one perspective, isn't the workplace simply an educational facility where employees learn the skills and knowledge necessary to do their jobs well? I think you will agree that the analogy is obvious. Over thirty-five years ago, research indicated clearly that a manager's expectations were a significant factor in the development of employees:

> Managers not only shape the expectations and productivity of subordinates but also influence their attitudes toward

their jobs and themselves . . . if they are skillful and have high expectations, subordinates' self confidence will grow, their capabilities will develop, and their productivity will be high.[62]

Perhaps this principle—that performance will generally rise to the level of our expectations—is a universal one. Nearly two hundred years ago, renowned poet and novelist Johann Wolfgang von Goethe said much the same thing: "If you treat an individual as he is, he will stay as he is; but if you treat him as if he were what he ought to be and could be, he will become what he ought to be and could be."[63]

1-on-1 Principle™: In a positive work environment, employees will rise to the level of the manager's expectations.

Key Expectations

We have established the general idea of "aligning expectations," but what exactly are we talking about? What specific expectations need to be discussed with employees?

The first set of expectations are those discussed above—that all employees can be successful and are expected to perform well, and that success is a part of the corporate culture. If this is not the case where you are a manager, then one of your first priorities is to begin to develop that environment for your employees; begin the process of raising the bar and raising the level of expectation. But be careful! It is not enough for a manager simply to say that he or she expects success—a manager's words and actions have to continually reinforce this cultural tenet. A manager must provide the means and opportunity for each individual employee to be successful and sincerely care about the development of those employees.

There are other critical expectations that must be communicated to each employee. First, each employee must understand what "success" is; in other words, what level of performance is the standard for the position? Secondly, each employee should understand how, and how frequently, performance is measured. Finally, each employee should be clear as to why their individual work is valuable to the company.

Expectation No. 1: Performance Standards

If team members don't understand the team's standards of performance, they will have nothing to aspire to, no benchmark to eclipse. In fact, if your team or department is new or recently formed, part of the team's job will be to jointly establish what each team member is expected to contribute to the team's success and what the standards of performance will be.

Dynastic sports teams and elite military units provide excellent examples of organizations that communicate standards of performance effectively. For example, in order to even receive consideration as a potential candidate to join the Navy SEALs, an applicant must complete the following Physical Screen Test (PST):

- Swim 500-yards using breast and/or sidestroke in less than 12 minutes and 30 seconds. 10-minute rest.

The Power of Expectations

- Perform a minimum of 42 push-ups in 2 minutes. 2-minute rest.

- Perform a minimum of 50 sit-ups in 2 minutes. 2-minute rest.

- Perform a minimum of 6 pull-ups (no time limit). 10-minute rest.

- Run 1½ miles wearing running shoes and shorts in under 11 minutes.[64]

These are the minimum standards that must be met by any applicant in order to even be considered for SEAL training. If accepted, each applicant undergoes rigorous training and further testing, including the final phase of SEAL training, which requires a successful candidate to complete a difficult obstacle course in ten minutes, run four miles in boots in thirty minutes, complete a fourteen-mile run, and swim two miles in the ocean with fins in seventy-five minutes. Failure to achieve these standards of performance disqualifies an individual from joining the SEALs.

These stringent standards are established for a very good reason. A typical SEAL operation might include free-fall parachuting from 10,000 feet, traveling by a small rubber boat for 100 miles, conducting a covert mission, and then traveling 30 miles out to sea to rendezvous with a submarine.[65] The mission results are usually critical, and the outcome of the operation usually affects the lives of many people, including the members of the SEAL team.

The critical observation here is that these rigorous standards don't deter those that want to be the very best at what they do. Instead, the standards challenge individuals to perform beyond their own expectations; they attract the very best applicants and ensure that those who are a part of the team are, indeed, highly qualified.

The same principle will apply in the workplace, but it doesn't matter what type of organization we discuss. High-performance individuals want to work in an environment where excellence is expected and the standards are high. In addition, when the standards of performance are well known and understood, the process of managing people becomes a little easier. Feedback is relative to a performance level that is already established—it doesn't come as a surprise. Performance review is not capricious or subjective, but based on pre-established standards. Employees always have a goal to aspire to and highly motivated employees will want to raise the bar even further!

1-on-1 Managers™ ensure that the answers to each of the following questions regarding performance standards are always known by the team as a whole, and by each individual on the team:

- What performance benchmarks are used in my position?
- What are the minimum standards of performance for my work?
- What constitutes excellence?
- What performance level represents the top 10 percent?
- What do I need to do to be the very best in my position?

Expectation No. 2: Performance Measurement and Review

Once standards of performance are established, it is important for each employee to know what metrics are used to assess that performance. Is it a production measurement? Is it a quality ratio? Is it the number of add-on sales? Whatever the measurement, it needs to be made available on a regular basis—daily, weekly, monthly, or quarterly—and it needs to be reviewed with the employee on a quarterly basis at a minimum.

So many organizations create sizeable problems for themselves simply because they rely on an annual performance review for employees. Sub-par performance is allowed to persist for months without being addressed adequately simply because the review process is flawed (more on this in chapter 11). It is difficult to provide an accurate and fair assessment of twelve months of employee performance in a single sixty- to ninety-minute review, and in many corporations, the annual process itself is poorly designed:

> Gallup consultants are often asked to statistically validate performance appraisal ratings against objective performance criteria. In many cases, the ratings don't correlate in any meaningful way to measurable outcomes. Often, there is no correlation, or worse, a negative one. In some cases, employees with the highest performance levels received the lowest ratings, and as a result, the least rewards. The end result is that the system weeds out top performers while rewarding mediocre ones.

1-on-1 Management

Why does this happen? Because manager ratings are inherently subjective—and this subjectivity only increases when the appraisals are linked to financial incentives such as merit pay raises. In one company, employees referred to the performance appraisal as "that form you need to fill out to give a person a raise."[66]

The objectives of the performance review should be to accurately assess work skills and production, to make adjustments as necessary, to acknowledge and reward superior work, and to provide input to the employee as to career direction and opportunities. In some cases, sub-par performance needs to be addressed and corrected. Wouldn't you rather address those issues after three months rather than waiting until the end of the year?

An effective performance review methodology incorporates outcome-focused measurements that "help focus every person, team, department, and business unit on driving performance and results."[67] Managing performance reviews this way "encourages an ongoing dialogue between managers and employees,"[68] a process that we will find to be a vital part of effective 1-on-1 Management™.

Conducting periodic staffing reviews gives management teams the opportunity and discipline to discuss their company's top and bottom performers, how to support and develop their top players, and how to deal with the ones who under perform.[69]

1-on-1 Managers™ ensure that the answers to the following

questions regarding performance review are always known by the team as a whole, and by each individual on the team:

- How am I graded?

- What performance measures are used to assess my performance?

- How often is performance reviewed with the team and with the employee?

- Where can the team and individual employees access the performance metrics?

Expectation No. 3: Contribution to Corporate Objectives

It is surprising how often employees have little idea how their jobs contribute to the objectives of the company. Each year, the owner or the executive team or the department manager spends considerable time developing budgets and performance objectives for the team but spends little time, if any, communicating those objectives to the team members.

In many cases, employers have done everything possible to eliminate critical thinking from the workplace by spelling out job descriptions in extreme detail. Call center employees are given scripts to memorize with little understanding of the problems they are asked to solve. Customer service employees are given policies to follow that often times insult a customer's intelligence. The worst example imaginable is the employee who proudly declares, "I did my job!" even though a customer or a large order is lost—all because organizations lose sight of the fact that every position and every job must be linked directly to the company's key objectives.

I have seen it more times than I care to count. Employees often refuse to do things that will directly affect a customer simply because it is not in their job description. Or, an employee will fail to act in a customer's interest because he or she will be scolded for failing to follow policy. The worst corporate offenders are often those companies that trumpet their loyalty to the customers and their dedication to "providing the best customer service." Don't believe me? Access the Internet and input "customer service horror stories" into your favorite search engine.

In every position in the company, the employee should understand clearly how their job relates to their customer, or customers, and the impact that their individual actions may have on that customer. Every employee should know clearly what the most significant key result areas are for the company and for their department in particular. Not dozens of objectives—three or four at the very most.

1-on-1 Managers™ ensure that the answers to the following questions regarding corporate objectives are always known by the team as a whole, and by each individual on the team:

- How does my job relate to the ultimate mission and critical objectives of the company?

- How does my work directly affect service or support of the customer, sales of the company's product or service, or quality or safety measures?

- How does my work contribute to the company's key result areas?

Conclusion

Great managers understand the vital importance of good communication, and they are acutely aware of the extent to which alignment of expectations is an integral part of that communication process. We have detailed three areas of expectation—each with its own set of questions. You shouldn't expect to answer these questions all at once, nor should you expect to answer them all on the employee's first day on the job. However, establishing each of these expectations is vital to creating a high performance team.

Every employee on your team should know what you expect regarding performance, and it is important to have high expectations simply because talented employees will stretch to meet those expectations *if* you lead them well. Every employee should also know exactly how their individual job contributes to the overall objectives of the company. Ensure that you connect his or her work directly to product quality, customer satisfaction, stakeholder value, or whatever mission-critical factors are determined by the company. In this way you make them an essential part of the organization.

Finally, every employee should know exactly how performance is measured; it is not enough to know what the standards are—performance must be measured against those standards. This is the only way that employees are able to determine exactly how they match up to your expectations, and it is an essential factor in creating accountability in the workplace.

In addition to the questions associated with these critical areas of expectation, there are four primary questions that every manager must answer for each and every employee. We will deal with those questions—and the right answers—in the next two chapters.

1-on-1 Insights™

- Employees don't suddenly get stupid when they join the company. If you repeatedly tell job candidates how talented they are and how good it will be to have them on board, and then treat them as if they can't do anything right once they start, you will lose their trust in a hurry.

- Employees will rise to the level of the manager's expectations, assuming they are given the opportunity.

- If you fail to establish expectations for the results you expect, or if you fail to create appropriate performance measures, it is extraordinarily de-motivating to an employee if you harshly criticize his or her performance. On the other hand, when your expectations are clear and employees know exactly how they are measured, it is difficult for them to avoid the obvious.

- Tie every job to the company's mission and strategic objectives. Make sure that each employee knows how he or she contributes to the company's success.

Four Key Questions Every Manager Must Answer (Part 1)

Talented employees want to be on a great team

> "The essence of competitiveness is liberated when we make people believe that what they think and do is important—and then get out of their way while they do it."
>
> —Jack Welch

Employees usually begin a new job with high hopes and expectations and with a positive, or at least neutral, level of trust for the company. As we discussed in chapter 6, establishing and communicating expectations is a key component in creating engagement and commitment to the company, but, at the same time, those actions begin the process of allowing an employee to develop trust in the manager. Great managers understand that trust is the cornerstone of leadership influence and the key to creating maximum performance.

1-on-1 Principle™: Employees will not exert maximum performance for a manager (or company) that they do not trust.

Trust is not only critical to employee loyalty and commitment, it has also been directly linked to corporate profitability, as evidenced by findings in a 2002 WorkUSA study:

Three-year total returns to shareholders (TRS) rates are significantly higher at companies with high trust levels, clear linkages between jobs and objectives, and employees who believe the company manages change well.[70]

The same study found that only 39 percent of employees in American companies trusted their senior management. Further, only 31 percent of employees rated their companies satisfactorily in the area of communication, although it was shown that "companies with HR functions that employees perceive as effective are more likely to have dramatically better trust levels, communication, commitment levels, and lines of sight."[71] [*Note: "Line of sight" is the term used to indicate the perception of the connection between an employee's job and the company objectives—one of the key expectations we discussed in chapter 6.*]

Communication and Trust

There are several things that impact whether we develop trust in someone: if their actions are consistent with their words, if they do the things they say they will do, if they do the right things regardless of consequences, if they treat people fairly, how they talk about (or don't talk about!) other people, and how they value others. As a manager, you should always be aware that your conduct is constantly being observed and your

—— Four Key Questions Every Manager Must Answer (Part 1) ——

communication is constantly being monitored. Your actions, your words, and your decisions send countless unspoken messages to the people that work for you.

Trust is a function of good communication, and it is vital for every manager to recognize that not all of our communication is verbal. We consistently communicate our principles and values through words *and* actions. In *Leading Change*, John Kotter writes:

> Communication [is] both words and deeds. The latter is generally the most powerful form. Nothing undermines change more than behavior by important individuals that is inconsistent with the verbal communication. And yet this happens all the time, even in some well-regarded companies.[72]

In his autobiography, *It Doesn't Take a Hero*, General Norman Schwarzkopf describes an event that illustrates this thought perfectly. As a colonel in Vietnam in 1970, Schwarzkopf received a report that one of the companies under his command had wandered into an unmarked mine field. One of his men had stepped on a land mine, and then another, and the troops began to panic. One of the men who had been hit was thrashing around on the ground, wounded, screaming, and creating further panic among the soldiers. Schwarzkopf was worried that the man would complicate his injuries or even detonate another mine, killing or wounding additional troops. Determining that immediate action was needed to maintain calm, and to prevent the situation from turning from bad to worse, he moved as quickly as he could to the injured man and pinned him down, lashing the man's wounded leg to his other leg with a belt.

1-on-1 Management

However, before Schwarzkopf could stabilize the situation, another mine exploded, seriously wounding a soldier and sending shrapnel into Schwarzkopf's chest. Wounded, and still working to calm the man he had reached, Schwarzkopf directed engineers to clear paths for his men to safely withdraw. Eventually, the men were extracted from the area, and Schwarzkopf was flown to a hospital.

After having his wounds treated, Schwarzkopf was making his way to the recovery room to check on the other injured men when three black soldiers stopped him in the hallway to thank him, and he remembers it this way:

"Colonel, we saw what you did for the brother out there," one said. "We'll never forget that, and we'll make sure that all the other brothers in the battalion know what you did." I was stunned. It hadn't registered on me until that moment that the kid in the minefield was black.[73]

As is often said, actions speak louder than words—especially the actions of a leader. Military officers are constantly judged not only by what they say, but by the actions they take on behalf of their troops. A former Navy SEAL offers this appraisal about the person in charge of a team:

You're a leader. Your people are watching you every time they see you. They're looking at every action, every moment. When they don't see you, they assume that you're working on their behalf. When they do see you, what you do confirms or destroys their assumptions.[74]

―――― Four Key Questions Every Manager Must Answer (Part 1) ――――

Managing Your Messages

Our messages are not limited to the words we speak; they take on other forms as well. For instance, the way in which you react to stress or failure sends a clear message to your employees. The way you recognize, or do not recognize, performance sends another message. If you are a poor communicator it is left to your employees to interpret what your lack of communication means. Are you simply an unskilled communicator, or are you secretive and manipulative?

If you neglect to praise top performers, your employees get the message. Your failure to dismiss poor performers also sends a loud and clear signal. How you allocate resources, whom you involve in critical decisions, the way you do or do not encourage your people, whom you include in meetings, how much latitude employees are given to perform their duties, whether or not you live according to the values you advocate—all of these actions create messages in the minds of employees.

In May 2006, *Harvard Business Review* published an article that described the consequences of unclear or inconsistent communication:

> ... think of the way a high-reliability team—say, an emergency room staff or a SWAT team—works. Every member has a precise understanding of what things mean. Surgeons and nurses speak the same medical language. SWAT teams know exactly what weapons to use, and when and how and under what conditions to use them. In these professions, there is absolutely no room for sloppy communication. If

team members don't speak to each other with precision, people die. People don't die in corporations, but without clear definitions and direction from the top, they work ineffectively and at cross-purposes.[75]

Clearly, any organization or department will suffer if the manager sends conflicting or unclear messages, and it is important to recognize that communication extends far beyond the spoken word. It is difficult enough to communicate effectively in person, with perceptions and intent often at odds with one another, but as we discussed in chapter 5, electronic messaging often replaces face-to-face communication—with disastrous results.

Most managers have little, if any, training in conflict resolution (yet another aspect of communication), which is remarkable when you consider that managing people frequently involves conflict. Unfortunately, for many managers (and many employees), electronic messaging has become the tool of choice for dealing with conflict. Worse, electronic messaging emboldens people to say things they would never say to someone in person. As a result, conflicts often spiral out of control without a word being spoken.

Here is one of the best pieces of practical management advice you will ever receive: if you are upset, angry, or disappointed, you should never discuss issues by e-mail or voice mail! Why? Because there is no dialogue, you cannot clarify intent, and it is quite difficult to convey your true feelings in an electronic message. Further, it is exceedingly difficult to change someone's mind—when emotions are running high—with an electronic message. It is human nature to interpret written words in light

─── Four Key Questions Every Manager Must Answer (Part 1) ───

of the opinions you have already formed about an issue rather than trying to neutrally interpret and understand the sender's actual intent.

A Manager's Four Critical Messages

When employees arrive on the job, they have four questions that they would like you to answer:

1. Who are we?

2. What is my job?

3. What kind of manager are you?

4. What opportunities do I have?

Sports teams provide a perfect example of this process. New players joining a team quickly adapt to the norms and characteristics of the team (who are we?) and learn exactly how they are expected to contribute (what is my job?). Within a short period of time, the new player will have a good idea of how the coach runs things (what kind of manager are you?). The last question—and most important to the real competitor—is "Will I get the chance to show what I can do?" Good coaches, as we will see illustrated later in the chapter, strive to create powerful team identities in which every team member contributes. Great coaches answer these four questions very clearly for every player because productive team dynamics depend on it.

As we discussed in chapter 6, aligning expectations is the first step in building trust between the manager and the employee, and each of these four questions relates to those expectations.

1-on-1 Management

Question 1: Who Are We?

Early in the interview process, most candidates begin to ask questions designed to find the answer to this question. They want to get a sense of the company's culture and work ethic. They want to know what sets the company apart. Because talented employees often have choices about where to go to work, they want to pick a good team—a team that will provide the opportunity for them to do good work and show off their skills.

1-on-1 Principle™: Talented employees want to be a part of something special; they want to play on a winning team.

One of the significant ways to answer the question "Who are we?" is to develop an identity for the team—a compelling reason to be a part of the team. In fact, a team or corporate *identity* speaks volumes about why a candidate should join the organization.

In sports, an identity includes things like a team logo, specific colors, team history, past championships, legendary players, traditions, and so on. The corporate world is not much different: logos (the Dallas Cowboys star), brands (iPod), specific colors (UPS and IBM, for example), corporate heritage, patents and inventions, market position, and so forth.

In the U.S. military, you can become one of "The Few. The Proud. The Marines." At Notre Dame, you don't run onto the field without touching a blue and gold sign that says "Play Like a Champion Today." For the New York police and fire departments, it is simply a hat with NYPD or FDNY emblazoned on the front that reminds us of the honor and significance of those organizations. For many young baseball players, the dream is to wear the pinstripes of Major League Baseball's New York Yankees. At Southwest Airlines, employees wear uniforms reflecting corporate colors and are encouraged to use humor on flights—a recognized trademark of Southwest Airlines personnel.

However, the one characteristic of each of these organization—the Marines, Notre Dame, NYPD or FDNY, the Yankees, or Southwest Airlines—is the reputation of excellence and high performance. Identity may begin with logos, colors, and uniforms, but it will never be an identity that consistently attracts talented employees until it is tied to outstanding performance. Talented employees want to know that they are part of something special—that they are part of a team with big goals, meaningful objectives, and a track record of success. The principle is exactly the same in the sports world, where great players prefer to play on championship caliber teams.

Savvy managers strive to develop an identity for their team that begins with a reputation for excellence and accomplishment. When new employees join the team, they realize that they have an opportunity to be a part of something special, and the opportunity to add to the team's legacy.

A Clear and Elevating Goal

A critical element in building an identity for an organization is the concept of a clear and elevating team objective. In 1989, Larson and LaFasto's research determined that the common element to high-performing teams was a *clear and elevating goal that unified and challenged the team.*

1-on-1 Management

First, high performance teams have both a clear understanding of the goal to be achieved and a belief that the goal embodies a worthwhile or important result. Second, whenever an *ineffectively* functioning team was identified and described, the explanation for the team's ineffectiveness involved, in one sense or another, the goal. The goal had become unfocused...[76]

Employees want to believe that they are a part of something with purpose, something that drives them to excel. Your team needs a vision—a clear and elevating goal—and each employee desperately wants to be a significant contributor to that objective. People need to be valued in their work in order to maintain morale, fuel performance, and create accountability.

Lieutenant Commander Jon Cannon, former Navy SEAL and co-author of *Leadership Lessons of the Navy SEALS*, understands the need for a clear and compelling purpose for the team:

People generally don't enjoy working in the dark. After all, you don't. If the only view someone has of the company is the four walls of their cube or office, then that's the extent of their concerns. If they know they're a part of something bigger, if they know how much their work matters and how it fits into the big picture, they're going to treat their work accordingly.[77]

Whether the objective is to attain six sigma quality standards, become the low-cost producer, set an all-time sales

—— Four Key Questions Every Manager Must Answer (Part 1) ——

record, own the largest market share, produce four new product innovations each year, achieve a perfect safety record, declare a dividend every quarter, reach profitability, or achieve any other objective, it must be communicated clearly and consistently to the team.

These objectives unify the team, focus the work effort, and provide the incentive for each employee to pursue excellence.

A Contrast in Identities and Objectives

In 2000, the New England Patriots hired Bill Belichik, the New York Jets' defensive coordinator, as their head coach. After a rocky debut season in 2001 (5-11), Belichik led the Patriots to Super Bowl wins in three of the next five years, compiling a regular season record of 58-22 over that span. Incredibly, all six first-round draft picks from 2001 through 2005 are currently starters for the team, while 2006 first-round pick Laurence Maroney contributed significantly in his rookie season.

Obviously, Belichik has excelled at finding great players and putting them into positions to succeed. At the same time, he believes strongly in his team's identity:

> I think it's more a function of the team than it is the individual. The essence of a team is that you really want to do something because all your friends and teammates are counting on you. You don't want to let the other guy down. It's more of a military philosophy. Any team that's good, that's really where the motivation is. In the end, when you have a commitment to each other, that's really where the power is.[78]

1-on-1 Management

The Patriots under Belichik have forged a strong identity, one grounded in the belief that they can and will go to the Super Bowl—an identity that is based on the principles of teamwork and excellence. "Teamwork is the ability for you to count on somebody else," said Belichik in a May 3, 2004 interview with the *Hartford Courant*. "We have a term: 'one die, all die.'"[79]

Contrast the Patriots with the downtrodden Detroit Lions. The fabled Lions won three world championships in the 1950s behind quarterback Bobby Layne, but haven't won a play-off game since a 38-6 triumph over the Cowboys in 1991. Since winning the 1957 NFL championship, the Lions have but that single playoff victory to their credit. Searching to repair a battered and beaten ship, the Lions hired former NFL player and erstwhile TV announcer, Matt Millen, to serve as the team's General Manager.

Millen assumed leadership of the organization prior to the 2001 season, and in the ensuing six years, the Lions have accumulated a mere 24 wins while losing 72 times (the Pats are 70-26 during the same period) and finished last in their division four times. From 2002 to 2006, the Lions lay claim to the worst record in the NFL, 22-58—worse even than the expansion Houston Texans who entered the league in 2002.

From 2001 to 2006, the Lions have had two No. 2 draft picks, a No. 3 draft pick, and three other top 10 picks, and they have used them to choose a quarterback, two wide receivers, a running back, and an offensive guard. Despite the additions to the team, the Lions have averaged only 17.5 points per game in Millen's tenure. The Patriots? Twenty-four points per game—almost a full touchdown better.

It has been nearly impossible for the Lions to build any

semblance of a team identity. Millen hired his third different head coach in five years prior to the 2006 season, but struggled to win only three games, their worst showing since 2002. In a news conference on November 29, 2005, Millen said, "We have not lived up to our expectations. We have underachieved as a football team."[80]

There has been no shortage of critics for Millen, who steadfastly refuses to step aside despite ongoing protest from fans.

"This has been going on for too long... You do take on a culture of your leadership. And it lingers and can hang around a long time. When Matt Millen came in, all of a sudden the team takes on the character of who is in charge. You cannot escape it."[81]

Which team would you prefer to play for?

Question 2:
How do I contribute to the team's success?

The second question that employees instinctively have pertains to their role in the company. Essentially, they want to know "What is my job and how does it help the company?" However, it is not the job description or the job requirements that are of great interest since that is usually self-evident. New employees generally receive a written or verbal job description, and they have a good idea of what the job requires. No, when an employee asks, "What is my job?" he or she wants to know what importance is attached to his/her contribution to the company.

1-on-1 Management

In fact, the second question (What is my job?) relates directly to the first question (Who are we?) because an employee wants to know specifically how they will contribute to the team's objectives *and* its identity:

- How do I contribute to the team's success?
- Am I a valued member of the team?
- Is my contribution important?
- How does my job relate to the big picture?

When a manager can clearly communicate a team member's value to the team and help the employee to comprehend how their contribution is a necessary part of the team's success, there is a greater connection to the organization. On the other hand, if an employee fails to gain a clear understanding of the way in which his or her job fits into the larger context of the organization, or the value that his or her job brings to the objectives of the team, the process of becoming disengaged and disconnected from the organization begins.

The Consequences of Isolation

Think about the worst job *you* ever had. In asking managers about their worst job experience, they invariably mention a manager first. Compensation, benefits, and working conditions are often mentioned as well, but the common culprit is almost always the manager. While there are many things a manager can do to discourage an employee, the common theme is a lack of perceived value on the part of the employee. For any number of reasons, the employee doesn't feel as if their work contribution is valued by the company.

As an employee becomes isolated from the big picture—unable to validate his or her contribution to the company's success—the lack of organizational perspective predictably shifts the employee's focus away from the team. I suspect that most every manager has heard an employee say, "I did *my* job." Indeed, I have witnessed situations where an employee said, "I did my job," when a customer or a sale was lost in the process!

The ensuing dialogue is remarkable:

Employee: "I did what I'm supposed to do. I finished the project."

Manager: "But we didn't get the completed project to the customer."

Employee: "Well, I put it on the Account Manager's desk."

Manager: "Didn't you know that the Account Manager was out sick?"

Employee: "Yes, but I didn't really think about that. My job was to get the project completed, and I did. The Account Manager's job is to get the project to the customer, not me. How can you be upset with me? I did my job."

Although it sounds completely absurd, I suspect every manager has heard some variation of this conversation at one time or another.

The Hidden Danger of Job Descriptions

As I mentioned, most jobs these days come complete with a job description—a formal document that outlines the employ-

1-on-1 Management

ee's responsibilities. It is produced in order to ensure that the employee understands everything he or she will be required to do in the position. In fact, job descriptions often contain a catch-all phrase that obligates the employee to complete "any and all other duties assigned by your manager or supervisor." However, while this document may be legally sound, it does little to instruct the employee as to how their position fits into the company's strategic plan or contributes to the company's objectives.

Experienced managers may have experienced another side of this issue. An employee focused only on their own individual work may become quite frustrated to learn, for example, that the company is not doing well—even as he or she completes their assigned tasks in an exemplary fashion. Jack Stack, president and CEO of SRC Holdings, Inc. (Springfield Remanufacturing Company), describes the positive consequences of showing employees the "big picture":

> Most of the problems we have in business today are a direct result of our failure to show people how they fit into the Big Picture. That failure undermines company after company. We put a guy in front of a radial drill and tell him to focus all his attention on drilling a hole as accurately as possible. So he does it. He drills the hole and he watches the forging go to the next station and he sees something fit perfectly into the hole he's just drilled. Then we come back and tell him the company is in trouble because there's something wrong with the way he's using his time. He can't understand. What could be wrong? His job was to drill the hole, and he did it perfectly. So if something is wrong, it has to be someone else's fault.[82]

Four Key Questions Every Manager Must Answer (Part 1)

When employees don't understand how the company functions, how the company makes money, how their work contributes to the profits of the company, and perhaps most importantly, how their work impacts the customer, they will struggle to understand how blame is shifted to them when things don't go well. Further, they won't feel like the team recognizes, or needs, their contribution to the process. That is why this message is so important.

Conclusion

The first two questions every manager must answer relate directly to the *identity* of the team: who are we, and how does each member contribute to the team's success? Identity is one of the cornerstones to creating high performance, and when each team member is sufficiently talented, properly trained, and linked together through a clear and elevating goal, teams can meet and exceed high expectations.

An excellent example of a composite team with specialized members is the United States Marine Corps fire team. Fire teams consist of four team members, each of whom has specific, mission-critical responsibilities: the rifleman, who also acts as scout; the team leader, who also serves as the grenadier; the automatic rifleman, who also serves as the second-in-command; and the assistant automatic rifleman, who carries additional ammunition. Typically, two fire teams will be grouped together to form a squad, and, although each fire team is equipped to act autonomously, they are generally deployed as a part of larger group operations. Members of a fire team develop tremendous camaraderie, and are often linked to larger elite units with their

1-on-1 Management

own culture, insignia, and combat history.[83]

When every member of your team knows how his or her position contributes to the overall succession of the team's mission, the team is poised to reach its potential. Your employees will begin to engage, and remain engaged, and team performance will steadily improve. The enduring benefit is that your team's success will contribute to its identity, and you will find it easier to attract and retain talent.

Only one person can really undermine your team at this point, and that is you, the manager. You still have to develop trust with your employees and create opportunities for them. You still have two more questions to answer effectively:

- What kind of manager are you?
- What opportunities do I have?

Words alone will not be enough. Remember, your actions—what you do and what you choose not to do—are an integral part of your communication.

1-on-1 Insights™

- Communication includes far more than what you tell your employees. It includes your actions, your decisions, and anything else you do that sends a message. If words and actions disagree—actions always win out.

- Start working on your team's identity. Winners want to play on a great team, and to attract the best employees, a manager must create a winning team.

Four Key Questions Every Manager Must Answer (Part 1)

- Connect the work of each position on your team directly to the mission and strategy of the company. Every employee should know exactly how their work contributes to the success of the company.

- Perhaps the biggest secret of team success is a clear and compelling objective for your team. Create one for your team, equip them to achieve it, and then get out of the way.

Four Key Questions Every Manager Must Answer (Part 2)

Trust is the key to creating maximum performance

"The absence of trust diverts the mental concentration and energy of a team away from its performance objective and onto other issues. The resulting loss of focus on the common goal is a critical factor. It wounds the team and often renders it ineffective."

—Carl E. Larson and Frank LaFasto,
Teamwork: What Must Go Right/What Can Go Wrong

You have begun to create an identity for your team. You have worked to foster that identity and to communicate it effectively to new employees. In addition, each employee has developed an understanding of how his or her individual job contributes to the success of the team.

Now what?

The next step is to prove yourself a capable leader. Remember, leadership is influence. Influence is determined by the level of trust developed in the relationship. Employees will quickly figure out if they can trust you, and one of the factors in that assessment is whether or not you allow them to do their jobs. If you are a control freak and feel compelled to micro-manage the

1-on-1 Management

details, you will find that 1) performance suffers, 2) employees disengage, and 3) turnover increases.

Two critical components to developing a high-performance team are to let employees do their jobs and to give them a clear line-of-sight to fulfilling their job and career objectives. That is what the next two questions are about.

Question 3: Do you trust me to do my job?

In answering this question, it is important to recognize that your actions and your words must be consistent or you will completely undermine your own efforts. In an effort to create a positive workplace environment, managers will often talk the talk of empowerment, but fail in the execution. While the intent is good—to allow employees to develop and use their talent and skills, and to make decisions and solve problems—it often turns out, sadly, to be empty rhetoric.

Let me stop for a minute and offer some clarification. Empowerment *never* means that employees are encouraged to do as they please in the workplace. Empowering employees is a skill to be learned, and it includes establishing appropriate boundaries and conditions for completing a task or project.

The military provides, perhaps, the very best example of how to do this effectively. In the highly acclaimed HBO series, *Band of Brothers*, viewers retrace the steps of Company E, one of five companies in the 101st Airborne's 506th Parachute Infantry Regiment. The tale of "Easy Company" begins during training at Camp Toccoa in Georgia, and viewers are introduced to the company's commanding officer (CO), Lieutenant Herbert Sobel. Sobel, portrayed by actor David Schwimmer, is depicted

Four Key Questions Every Manager Must Answer (Part 2)

as a tyrant, a petty man who fails miserably to win the respect of his troops as he trains them for combat.

Sobel's leadership failure is so demoralizing to Easy Company that a number of non-commissioned officers threaten to give up their stripes—in effect, to resign—rather than go into battle with him as their CO. As a result, Sobel is relieved of his command and replaced by 1st Lieutenant Thomas Meehan prior to the landing at Normandy. Sadly, Meehan is killed during the opening hours of the D-Day invasion, and the main character in the series, Lieutenant Dick Winters, assumes command of Easy.

Winters is competent, level-headed, and well-trained. His ingenuity and courage are vividly illustrated in the second episode in the series when he leads a D-Day assault against a battery of German 105 mm howitzers firing on Utah beach during the invasion.[84]

Winters is given the task to take out the German guns—but he is not told how to do the job. He has been trained and prepared for this type of mission, so the expectation is that he will be able to execute the attack successfully. It should be noted that, despite the importance of the mission, his every move is not directed by a group of higher-ranking officers. Rather, he is given the information available (enemy location, strength, etc.) and the materiel that he needs (armament and ammunition), and he chooses a dozen men with specific capabilities to complete the assignment. As the squad approaches the gun emplacements, Winters evaluates the field conditions and creates a plan to successfully neutralize the gun battery. His men carry out the attack brilliantly and successfully, and the German guns are neutralized, saving countless lives. The maneuver, referred to as the "Brécourt Manor Assault," earned Winters the Distinguished Service Cross, and is today still studied at West Point as a classic example of small unit tactics.

Managers who do not believe that employees can be trusted to complete critical assignments without micro-management need to look no further than military examples like these for confirmation. Here come the inevitable objections and questions. Do similar situations lead to failure in the field? Sure. Might Lieutenant Winters and his squad have failed in this mission? Absolutely. However, successful managers understand clearly that failures (and the lessons taught by failure) are necessary to produce high-performing teams.

Stop for a moment and envision a scenario where an officer accompanies the squad into battle and micro-manages every detail of the attack. Or, think about the situation that may have occurred if Winters felt compelled to do everything himself rather than rely on the expertise of his men. Speed and agility would be compromised, as tactical decisions would not be made by front-line troops under fire. Most importantly, employees (or soldiers) will not develop trust in the boss—which is illustrated vividly by Lieutenant Sobel's experience as the CO of Easy Company.

Rules and Regulations

Unquestionably, organizations need boundaries; hence, the need for guidelines, policies, procedures, rules, and regulations. Unfortunately, these rules are often constructed to control individual behavior so that managers won't be burdened with teaching and developing employees, or making critical decisions.

Four Key Questions Every Manager Must Answer (Part 2)

Kimray, Inc., a company located in Oklahoma City, was founded by Garman O. Kimmell in 1948 to produce control valves and related equipment for the oil and gas industry. Tom Hill, the president, was confronted with a dismal situation at Kimray in the early 90s. The company had a policy and procedure manual chock full of rules for governing employee behavior, but the company was still beset with employee drug problems, escalating workers' compensation costs, high employee turnover, and increasing employee absenteeism.

One morning it dawned on Hill that things were completely out of control at Kimray. He noted a rule in the company policy and procedure manual that prohibited employees from sitting on the tank portion of the restroom toilets. He couldn't fathom where such a rule could have originated, so he went to find out. What he discovered was that employees on the third shift (nights) had been caught sleeping in the restrooms—simply sitting down on a restroom toilet and taking a nap! Supervisors, upon learning this, would occasionally step into the restroom and bend down to look under the doors of the stalls to see if they could see someone's legs. Before long, however, employees caught on and took to sitting up on the tank portion of the toilet so supervisors wouldn't be able to see them. Hence, a new rule for the manual—with appropriate consequences, of course.[85]

1-on-1 Principle™: A manual full of rules is a poor substitute for hiring employees with good character and treating them well.

Certainly, this is an extreme case, but one that I use to illustrate how companies can become quite out of control in the

1-on-1 Management

quest to micro-manage performance *and* employee behavior. The biggest struggle that most managers deal with is employee empowerment—allowing employees to do their job without micro-managing the details. Indeed, many managers live by the adage, "If you want it done right, do it yourself." They can't or won't take the time to train and develop employees to do it right.

Sometimes, it is simply a lack of know-how. Many managers have been promoted due to their performance or specialized knowledge or technical skill, but they have never received any significant training in how to manage people. For others, it could be an inherent distrust in people, or it could be that some managers think it is too much work to teach someone else—they would rather just do it themselves. Still others find value—and take pride—in being "in charge," and feel compelled to take credit for what happens in their department.

No matter the cause, it is easy to spot the symptoms of micro-management: disengaged employees, high employee turnover, and consistently mediocre performance.

Employee Empowerment

Great managers quickly learn that the essence of management is not to fix problems and do everything themselves. The key to effective management is to unlock the potential of employees and trust them to do their jobs well. As author and educator Booker T. Washington once observed, "Few things help an individual more than to place responsibility upon him, and to let him know that you trust him."[86]

—— Four Key Questions Every Manager Must Answer (Part 2) ——

However, a manager cannot simply "empower" employees; empowerment is a process—one that is entirely dependent upon *trust*. Who will empower anyone, in any situation, unless adequate trust has been developed? This is the focus of 1-on-1 Management™; it is designed to provide the framework that allows you to create trust and thus empower your employees.

1-on-1 Principle™: Employee empowerment is a process that is completely contingent upon trust.

When you have capable employees, and mutual trust has been created, empowerment is a straightforward process:

- Communicate the results that you expect.
- Outline the boundaries and the level(s) of authority.
- Review and provide feedback as needed.

Micro-managers—or managers who fear employee failure—shudder at the thought of allowing employees to attack complex tasks without controlling every detail. However, great managers *expect* their employees to complete complex tasks, and to do so with excellent results.

Here is how: First, they clearly communicate the desired results as well as the expected time frame for completion. They do not make assumptions about the employee's understanding; instead, they ask questions to clarify understanding and ensure that success is well-defined. Jeff and Jon Cannon discuss this process specifically in their book, *Leadership Lessons of the Navy SEALS*:

1-on-1 Management

As a leader, communicating your mission means spelling out exactly what you want done . . . and when you want the results delivered. Doing this boldly and clearly reinforces the idea that you are in command, that you know what you're asking for, and that there is universal understanding of your task.[87]

Next, they define the boundaries and the level of authority. Boundaries mean exactly what the word implies—what the employee can do and what he or she cannot do. It provides the limits and necessary safeguards to task completion so that you are not required to oversee the details of the task. Boundaries might address the amount of money that can be spent, the resources that can or cannot be utilized, or the systems or processes that the project must integrate into. Boundary definitions always include *the time frame for completion*. The employee should very clearly understand your expectation for *when* the task or project will be completed.

Levels of authority refer to the decision-making process—the level of freedom that is provided for making decisions:

- Level 1: Ask permission before making any decision.

- Level 2: Make the decision, but confer with the manager prior to implementation.

- Level 3: Make and implement the decision, but inform the manager of the decision made (keeping the manager in the loop).

- Level 4: Make any and all decisions on your own with no outside involvement or responsibility. (The buck stops here!)

Four Key Questions Every Manager Must Answer (Part 2)

With the expected results, boundaries, and level-of-authority clearly communicated, an employee can proceed to use his or her skills and talents to complete any task or project. The only thing left to do is to review progress and provide feedback as needed. We will talk much more about performance feedback in chapter 10 when we discuss the 1-on-1 Meeting™.

There is one thing further to consider in the empowerment process—the way you respond to success, *and* the way you respond to failure. The correct response in either situation is absolutely critical to building and maintaining a high level of trust.

You already know that employees want to be valued (chapter 3), so success should be met with commensurate praise and recognition. Small victories don't merit the same response as major victories; but, in fact, even routine work should be acknowledged when it is done well (more on recognition in chapter 9).

At the same time, your reaction to *failure* can easily prevent any employee from reaching the highest levels of performance. If failure elicits negative reactions from you of any kind, from rolling your eyes to a full-blown temper tantrum, your employees will shy away from the empowerment process as much as the enthusiastic micro-manager. *Remember: failure, or less-than-stellar results, provides the perfect opportunity to coach.* We will look into this in great detail in chapter 11.

1-on-1 Management

Question 4:
Will I get the chance to develop my potential?

The final question that an employee wants answered relates directly to his or her future. In my experience, one of the questions that high-performance employees typically ask during the interview process is "What type of training do you provide?" The majority of prospective employees will also have questions about the criteria and opportunity for promotions, pay raises, or performance bonuses.

Companies and managers often overlook the fact that employees cannot, and will not, work at a top level of performance for any significant period of time without a clear objective in mind. In fact, one of the single biggest de-motivators in any endeavor, inside or outside the workplace, is to have no sense of an ultimate goal or objective to work towards. Alternatively, if the employee has a clear vision of success and is motivated by the consequences of that success, then high levels of performance can be sustained.

Providing the opportunity to develop potential may mean creating the opportunity to move up the corporate ladder, or it may relate to developing new skills, or it may mean assigning more complex and sophisticated projects. Regardless of what it means, it is critical for the manager to understand exactly what it is for every employee. Savvy managers help their employees get where they want to go.

Consider the world of sports. Have you seen an athlete who doesn't train with an objective in mind? While the reasons for training may vary dramatically—to lose weight, to improve specific skills, to improve overall health, to earn a position on a team, to win a championship—I have not observed anyone that works out consistently for no reason at all! In fact, it is not uncommon to see someone pay for the right to use an exercise facility and discontinue working out—in effect, forfeiting the investment—because they lose sight of their objectives!

For many years, physicians and athletes alike considered the four-minute mile an unbreakable barrier. Until Roger Bannister broke the tape in 3:59.4 at Oxford in 1954, the world was convinced that the human body was not capable of running that fast. Bannister, a young Oxford medical student, remained unconvinced. He applied all of his knowledge and training to a single goal—breaking the four-minute-mile barrier. In doing so, he stunned the world and crashed through a psychological barrier as well. Only forty-six days later, his greatest rival, John Landy, ran 3:57:9 in Finland. Within three years, sixteen different runners had reached a goal once considered impossible.

Would Bannister have worked that hard and remained that focused without a clear and compelling objective to drive his performance?

Career Development— A Key to Employee Engagement

For the athlete or the employee, it seems clear that objectives or goals are the primary drivers of performance. Those goals can be "end-result" goals (I want to become a manager) or "performance" goals (I want to reach $1 million in sales), but an end-result goal must always be supported by a performance goal. For example, Bannister's end-result goal might have been to be the fastest miler in the world, but without the performance goal—running a mile in four minutes or less—he couldn't know what was needed to reach that objective.

The performance goal creates the vital link to the work process. Just as a clear vision of running a four-minute mile motivated Bannister to train and push himself beyond his own expectations, a clear vision of reward or career advancement motivates the high-performance employee to strive for excellence each day in the workplace. The proverbial "light at the end of the tunnel" is what keeps an individual focused on success.

In their book, *First, Break All the Rules*, authors Coffman and Buckingham summarized years of workplace research conducted by the Gallup Organization. In this research, Gallup interviewed over 1 million employees on "every conceivable aspect of the workplace."[88] The responses to these questions enabled Gallup to discover twelve key questions to ask employees that effectively measure the strength of a workplace.[89] Not surprisingly, three of those twelve questions relate directly to an employee's career objectives:

- Is there someone at work who encourages my development?

- In the last six months, has someone at work talked to me about my progress?

- In the last year, have I had opportunities at work to learn and grow?

―― Four Key Questions Every Manager Must Answer (Part 2) ――

Gallup discovered that when they receive affirmative answers to a majority of all twelve questions, they could clearly identify an "engaging" work environment. With three of the twelve questions pertaining to career development, it is not unreasonable to conclude that as much as 25 percent of employee engagement is dependent upon your ability to help employees reach their career objectives.

We'll talk much more about career development in chapter 12 when we outline the 1-on-1 Development Plan™.

Conclusion

To create trust with employees, a manager must develop trust *in* employees. When given the opportunity to produce results, talented employees will do just that—produce. Unfortunately, many managers feel compelled to treat employees like children, micro-managing every detail of their work. Why? Because they might make a mistake; worse, they might fail.

Train your employees. Express confidence in their ability. Allow them to make mistakes—and *teach* them in the process. The parallels between athletic coaches and managers are remarkable (as we will discover in chapter 11), but most managers fail miserably at the all-important task of coaching, or teaching, their employees. The trust that will develop between you and your employees as you *teach* them will be remarkable, and their performance and productivity will dramatically improve as they gain confidence in their abilities.

1-on-1 Insights™

- Great employees don't want reins; they want to run. Give them an objective, define their boundaries and level of authority—then get out of the way.

- You cannot create rules for every possible situation. It is far easier to hire people with character and treat them like adults.

- No one does their best work in a dead-end situation. Give your employees a reason to excel and create opportunities for them to develop their career.

- You can empower your employees, but it won't happen overnight—it takes time to develop trust. It also takes courage to *learn to trust.*

Creating an Environment of Employee Engagement

Motivating employees is as simple as creating an engaging work environment

> "I have yet to find the man, however exalted his station, who did not do better work and put forth greater effort under a spirit of approval than under a spirit of criticism."
>
> —Charles Schwab

Stop for a moment and think back on your career. Remember the worst job you ever had? As you consider your worst experiences as an employee, think about the specific things that made you want to find a new job as soon as possible. Now write down three of those things in the space below:

1. _____
2. _____
3. _____

By now, you should realize that when an employee leaves a company, it is most often the result of how he or she has been treated by a manager. Remember the 1-on-1 Principle™ from

1-on-1 Management

chapter 2? Employees join companies, but they quit managers. Research certainly supports this concept. According to *The 7 Hidden Reasons Employees Leave*, 70 percent of the reasons cited by employees for quitting a job are directly related to the actions of an immediate supervisor.[90] In fact, this study revealed that 89 percent of *managers* believe that employees leave their companies for more money, when, in fact, 88 percent of *employees* actually leave for reasons other than money![91]

The odds, then, are pretty good that one of the three spaces above contains someone's name—most likely that manager you didn't care for—or at the very least, they contain three things about that specific manager that you did not like. Of course, there may have been other factors in your list: low pay, bad work hours, poor work environment, dull or unchallenging work, or a lack of opportunity, for example. However, in the majority of cases, it is a poor manager that is the focal point of a bad work experience.

What do these ineffective managers do wrong? They criticize in public. They take credit for work they don't do themselves. They fail to thank employees for sacrifices made to get things done. They don't do what they say they will do. They don't treat employees fairly. They don't listen.

Like clockwork, the same answers come out over and over. Consider these behaviors cited in a recent Florida State University survey of more than 700 employees:

- 31 percent of respondents reported that their supervisor gave them the "silent treatment" in the past year.

- 37 percent reported that their supervisor failed to give credit when due.

—— Creating an Environment of Employee Engagement ——

- 39 percent noted that their supervisor failed to keep promises.

- 27 percent noted that their supervisor made negative comments about them to other employees or managers.

- 24 percent reported that their supervisor invaded their privacy.

- 23 percent indicated that their supervisor blamed others to cover up mistakes or minimize embarrassment.[92]

Not only is it commonplace for managers to be unprepared for the challenges of leading employees, but it is also not at all uncommon for managers to treat employees unprofessionally. The FSU study also concludes that there is a direct link between the adverse behaviors listed and a negative impact on the health and job performance of employees.

No kidding?

Whose Fault is it Any Way?

By now, you should be acutely aware that the person responsible for the performance and commitment of your employees is *you*, the manager. After all, you hire them, you train them, you manage them, you lead them, you set the expectations, and your behavior is the example they see every day. If they aren't performing adequately, we can come to one of two conclusions: either you aren't hiring the right people or you are not an effective leader. Either way, it is time to look squarely at yourself and quit blaming your employees!

1-on-1 Principle™: The actions of a manager primarily determine the employee's level of engagement and commitment to the company.

Look closely inside any organization—if you see any of the following warning signs, it is a clear indicator that there are leadership problems in the company: poor morale, lack of attention to detail, sub-par performance, finger-pointing and a lack of accountability, absenteeism, or employee turnover.

In fact, it is this last item—employee turnover—that leads us to the ultimate barometer for the health of a corporate culture: *employee engagement*. The *Gallup Management Journal*'s semi-annual Employee Engagement Index is an extensive survey of U.S. employees that reveals different levels of employee engagement: engaged, not engaged, and actively disengaged. The Gallup study reveals that a whopping 56 percent of the U.S. workforce are "not engaged," meaning the employees are in neutral and going nowhere fast. While these employees aren't hurting their companies intentionally, their productivity is far from what it would be if they were "engaged"— like the 29 percent of employees who are loyal, committed, and moving the organization forward.[93]

The more disturbing revelation in this study is that 15 percent of workers report they are *"actively* disengaged." This translates to more than 20 million employees who report that they are not only unhappy with their respective organization, but, according to Gallup, are also *actively undermining the efforts of their co-workers*! While the *disengaged* employee puts his or her work on cruise control and does little beyond the minimum acceptable standard, the *actively disengaged*

── Creating an Environment of Employee Engagement ──

employee can wreak havoc on the organization in any number of ways.

Going back to the research done in *The 7 Hidden Reasons Employees Leave*, author Leigh Branham analyzed the responses of more than 19,000 employees exiting their companies. He concludes that the core issues leading to employee disengagement and turnover are directly related to four fundamental human needs:

1. **The Need for Trust:** Expecting the company and management to deliver on its promises . . .

2. **The Need to Have Hope:** Believing that you will be able to grow, develop your skills . . . and have the opportunity for advancement . . .

3. **The Need to Feel a Sense of Worth:** Feeling confident that if you work hard, do your best, demonstrate commitment, and make meaningful contributions, you will be recognized and rewarded accordingly . . .

4. **The Need to Feel Competent:** Expecting that you will be matched to a job that makes good use of your talents . . .[94]

Quite simply, people want to be treated with dignity and respect—the workplace is no different than any other aspect of an employee's life. When basic psychological needs are left unfulfilled, it is simply unreasonable to assume that a company will receive the maximum performance from its employees. In fact, wherever possible, employees will begin to disengage from the company and look for other job opportunities.

Herein lies one of the significant threats to business. As of this writing, unemployment in the United States hovers

1-on-1 Management

around 4.5 percent and many market sectors are struggling to find capable, qualified employees. If talented employees aren't readily available, the only alternative is to poach employees from other companies. If your employees are disenchanted and disengaged, your company is a target-rich environment for your competitors!

A High-Performance Work Environment

To be clear, fulfilling an employee's "fundamental needs" should not to be perceived as some kind of weak-kneed, join-hands-and-sing-around-the-campfire approach to management. Quite the contrary, high-performance corporate cultures are demanding and based on personal accountability.

In his book, *Don't Fire Them, Fire Them Up,* Xerox sales manager Frank Pacetta describes how he successfully dealt with a classic case of employee disengagement. Accepting the challenge to turn around a lackluster, underperforming sales team in Cleveland, Ohio, in January 1988, Pacetta arrived to find a "culture of failure . . . so well established that even the winners saw themselves in a negative light."[95] Of the sixty-five Xerox sales districts in the United States, the one in Cleveland was consistently near the bottom in performance, with only twelve of the thirty-four sales representatives reaching their sales targets the previous year.

To turn around a division so mired in mediocrity required a radically new vision for the district, an entirely new identity for the sales team, and a culture markedly different from the one he inherited. Pacetta set out immediately to change the workplace atmosphere, making it clear that everyone would be

Creating an Environment of Employee Engagement

responsible for "paying the rent." He set minimum standards of performance, demanded accountability to those standards, and thoroughly inspected the details of every sales plan of every single salesperson.

Pacetta also went to great lengths to recognize and reward success, and he continually demanded that marginal performers step up—or step out. Throughout the process, he focused on building an environment of engagement. His actions allowed him to develop influence with the salespeople in the Cleveland district because he was fair, he was consistent, and he did everything he could to help his people be successful:

> You win with people if you cherish them, develop them, and show them that you sincerely care about their success. We either build trust, create loyalty, and generate enthusiasm, excitement, and teamwork, or step to the sidelines and watch history and the competition pass us by.[96]

The results were stunning. Cleveland, a district that finished sixtieth out of sixty-five districts in profitability in 1987, vaulted to fourth the following year, and sales revenue climbed from $56 million to $100 million in a period of four years.[97]

Creating an Environment of Engagement

Creating an environment of engagement is, first and foremost, a function of treating your employees with dignity and respect. Any conversation about managing people must begin there. Human nature is such that people expect to be treated respectfully—on the job or anywhere else—and it is not possible to create goodwill and develop trust in employees while treating them otherwise.

Unfortunately, in an effort to control employee behavior, managers frequently treat people in ways that are neither dignified nor respectful. Some managers, for example, use intimidation as their primary means of getting what they want. They bully their employees into submission and work hard to make sure everyone knows "who the boss is around here." There are also managers who use fear to create compliance, and still others who are guilty of using humiliation to manipulate their employees.

In other words, when managers don't know *how* to get employees to work for them, they have to find a way to *force* their employees to work for them. The bottom line is that you will never influence people until they trust you, and they will never trust you if you aren't trustworthy. In managing your employees, this means being fair, being consistent, and doing what you say you will do.

Simple enough. Be fair. Be consistent. Be honest.

Treating employees with dignity and respect helps to satisfy their need for *trust*. Next, we are left to address the other three needs Branham lists—the need to feel competent, the need to feel a sense of worth, and the need to have hope.

The Need to Feel Competent

To satisfy an employee's need to feel competent, a manager must ensure that his or her employees know how to do the basics of their job well. In other words, you should not make any assumptions about an employee's ability to do their

―――― Creating an Environment of Employee Engagement ――――

job—you should train them well and measure the results you care about. This is a critical, yet often overlooked, requirement of management. If your people haven't been trained to do their jobs well, it is impossible to hold them accountable to a standard of performance. Without accountability to a standard of performance, malaise rapidly sets into an organization, and employees begin to disengage.

This is exactly what Frank Pacetta found in the Cleveland district that he successfully transformed into a powerhouse for Xerox. Specifically, he discovered that sales reps in his district were not making the same number of sales calls as those in top-performing districts; they simply weren't getting their product in front of decision makers. Salespeople weren't out in the field making qualified sales calls or executing a well-devised strategic plan—the basics of successful selling.

Pacetta took immediate action, requiring specific weekly objectives in support of their sales plans. He required each rep to complete a minimum of four calls every day, and held them accountable to that standard. Further, he questioned every sales call and trained his managers to do the same. This ensured that the four sales calls were four *effective* sales calls.

I suspect that the idea of teaching the basics may seem elementary, but I am no longer surprised at how frequently I observe employees who do not perform the basic requirements of their jobs well. Investigation reveals a number of reasons for this: poor or non-existent training, inadequate employee orientation, a misunderstanding of job requirements, or a lack of accountability. However, none of these reasons have anything to do with the employee's ability; in fact, in each of these cases, the blame for failure can be placed almost everywhere *except*

1-on-1 Management

on the employee! How can you demand superior performance if your employees are inadequately trained or equipped?

General Norman Schwarzkopf recounts a number of his experiences as a colonel in Vietnam in his autobiography, *It Doesn't Take a Hero*. In one particularly instructive story, he describes this encounter with a group of soldiers who did not perform the most basic components of their jobs well despite the clear and present danger of direct contact with the enemy:

> Nothing was camouflaged . . . the guy who guided us in to land wore a pair of bright red shorts, flip-flops, and a yellow bandanna around his head, and had a three-day growth of beard. I jumped off and walked over to a lieutenant standing nearby—he had no helmet and no weapon, even though this was supposedly enemy territory . . .
>
> The captain came back—still wearing no helmet. "Sir, I don't have one," he explained . . .
>
> "Do you have security posted around your perimeter?"
>
> "Uh . . . yes, sir."
>
> "Okay, take me to it." We started walking into the bushes. As we moved further and further out, the captain was calling, "Security? Security?" After a couple of hundred yards, I said disgustedly, "We're wasting our time. Let's go back and ask your platoon leaders where security is . . ."
>
> The bottom line was that they had no security. The enemy could have strolled in, opened fire, and killed dozens of men. We retraced our steps and I inspected the camp itself.

Creating an Environment of Employee Engagement

> I walked up to a machine gunner whose weapon had no bullets in it and was coated with rust. When I asked why the gun wasn't loaded he hung his head and explained that his ammunition was in his rucksack. I wasn't angry with him—it was his sergeant who was responsible—but I said, "Okay, soldier. Let's do a simulation. You're under attack. Get your ammunition." The guy scrambled over to his rucksack and turned it upside down. Out tumbled a portable radio, cans of food, books, and a hopeless tangle of ammunition belts, all rusty and caked with the crumbs of cookies from home.
>
> I knew I had to put an end to this carelessness before men started dying.[98]

It is difficult to believe that a group of soldiers in harm's way could be so cavalier about their protection—the most basic of a soldier's responsibilities—but it is even more implausible to believe that the officers in charge would allow conditions to deteriorate to the point described above.

As one might reasonably predict, the outgoing battalion commander—the man who allowed these conditions to exist—blamed everyone but himself. Schwarzkopf's meeting with him was brief:

> I was expecting a two- or three-hour discussion of the battalion, its officers, its NCOs, its mission, but he only said, "Well, I hope you do better than I did. I tried to lead as best I could, but this is a lousy battalion. It's got lousy morale. It's got a lousy mission. Good luck to you." With that he shook my hand and walked out.[99]

1-on-1 Management

A workplace environment of accountability, one in which employees take responsibility for results, is nearly impossible to create if individual employees are not well-trained and fully aware of the requirements and expectations of the job. However, once trained, and aware of your expectations, employees are quite capable of fulfilling their need to feel competent.

The Need to Feel a Sense of Worth

To satisfy an employee's need to feel a sense of worth, a manager must make recognition and encouragement a core part of his or her leadership style. Employee recognition is like throwing fuel on a fire—more fuel means a larger fire and more heat, but in the absence of adequate fuel, the fire eventually dwindles out.

I am indebted to a good friend who introduced me to a terrific book written by James Kouzes and Barry Posner entitled *Encouraging the Heart: A Leader's Guide to Rewarding and Recognizing Others*. In this powerful book, the authors report that a staggering 98 percent of employees surveyed indicated that they perform at a higher level when they receive encouragement about their performance.[100]

There is more clear evidence that recognition is an incredibly powerful managerial tool—a tool that can have a profound impact on an organization. The Jackson Organization and authors Adrian Gostick and Chester Elton analyzed survey data from 26,000 employees who were asked to rank their agreement with this statement: "My organization recognizes excellence." The results from this survey are nothing short of incredible. For the top 25 percent of companies with employees

———— Creating an Environment of Employee Engagement ————

claiming the highest level of agreement with that statement, the companies not only had lower employee turnover, but they also experienced significantly better financial results, including return-on-equity, return-on-assets, and operating margins.[101]

Great managers realize that recognition is one of the most important assets in creating a high-performance team, and it doesn't even cost the company money. It does, however, require an investment in time, but that investment yields incredible returns—not only in lower employee turnover, but also significant improvements in measurable financial results.

In many cases, the vast improvements in employee turnover alone often results in enormous savings to the company. For a company with 200 employees and 20 percent employee turnover annually, the nominal cost to the company—assuming a pay rate of only $8.00 per hour—would be $140,000 annually using the lowest available estimate of the costs associated with employee turnover. The average turnover cost of an $8.00 per hour employee—using the 10 lowest estimates available—is $5,505, which results in a loss of $220,200 annually. Lowering employee turnover to 10 percent would save the company over $100,000 per year![102]

While mediocre managers believe that pay raises and better benefits are the only way to motivate employees, this data clearly indicates that recognition and encouragement can have an extraordinary impact on an organization. It is important, however, to understand that the type of recognition that produces these kinds of results is much more than the typical "nice job" or "way to go" offered by managers. In fact, even the best intentions may lead to disastrous consequences.

1-on-1 Management

Consider this story from *Encouraging the Heart*:

The president of one of my professional associations once brought me and a handful of volunteers on stage at the end of a convention where I had served as logistics chair. I expected, perhaps, a few sentences about the two years I'd served on the committee preparing for the event, the two cross-country flights I'd made at my own expense for committee meetings, the hundreds of hours I'd put in, and the one hundred volunteers I'd recruited and trained.

Instead, he said two sentences I'll never forget: "Rebecca did the little things. If no one else would do it, we knew Rebecca would." I was stunned, crushed. It sounded like I'd collated a few packages, or made some copies. I could barely see my sixteen hundred colleagues giving us a standing ovation. When I got off stage, I had to leave the room. I cried for an hour. He had meant well; he just didn't think about it until we were on stage. Now, I know that when I acknowledge someone—I need to be clear on "How can I phrase this, to leave the person feeling honored, not diminished?"[103]

Clearly, there is a skill involved in recognizing employees. Unquestionably, doing it right strengthens the organization. Doing it wrong can lead to further deterioration in morale. The lesson is that those managers that do offer encouragement and recognition may dilute the full impact of recognition by failing to make the recognition personal, specific, and meaningful. Gostick and Elton outline a very effective recognition program in their book *The Carrot Principle*:

––––––– Creating an Environment of Employee Engagement –––––––

First, link recognition to your company and team goals. You'll want to reinforce what matters most—the *values* of the organization. Next, for the greatest *impact*, present awards that match the level of the contribution and the interests of the employees being honored. Finally, make the presentation of awards *personal* and meaningful to the employees. In presenting an award, tell a specific, informed story about the accomplishment.[104]

Recognizing achievement is perhaps the most powerful tool that a manager has at his or her disposal, but a random or haphazard approach to using this tool is ill-advised. A manager should carefully plan each time an employee is recognized publicly to maximize the impact.

- Tell a detailed story about the accomplishment; bring the story to life.

- Connect the accomplishment to a corporate value or strategic objective that you want to reinforce.

- Take care to use the appropriate award for the level of impact the accomplishment had on your organization.

- Make it personal; shake the employee's hand (or put a hand on their shoulder, for example), and thank them publicly for their commitment to the organization.

Along with recognition, great managers also use encouragement to engage employees—everything from a verbal "Well done!" or "Nice work" to a written note or e-mail message. Some managers have found that a simple note of encouragement can have a profound effect on employees, and that may be true for no other reason than the fact that many people have been criticized all of their lives and rarely, if ever, have been encouraged or praised for their efforts.

The Need to Have Hope

Finally, to satisfy an employee's need to have hope, a manager must provide employees with the opportunity to achieve success and advance their careers.

When you set the bar high and challenge your employees to leap over, you provide opportunities to build confidence and increase job satisfaction. Generally, employees find considerable value in achievement or superior accomplishment, and there is great satisfaction in completing an important project, solving a significant problem, or overcoming a challenge.

In their article, "Inner Work Life," Teresa Amabile and Steven Kramer detail a research project in which 238 employees from 26 project teams were asked to complete journal entries recording their inner thoughts on the work accomplished each day. The intent of the study was to determine the actual perceptions, emotions, and motivations that employees experience in the workplace. The results reinforce the old notion that "success breeds success":

> When people are blocked from doing good, constructive work day by day, for instance, they form negative impressions of the organization, their co-workers, their managers, their work, and themselves; they feel frustrated and unhappy; and they become de-motivated in their work. Performance suffers in the short run, and in the longer run, too. But when managers facilitate progress, every aspect of

──── Creating an Environment of Employee Engagement ────

people's inner work lives are enhanced, which leads to even greater progress. This positive spiral benefits the individual workers—and the entire organization."[105]

Read that again, closely. One of the keys to creating an engaged workforce is to let people do their jobs. Get out of the way! Facilitate progress. Give your employees the opportunity to succeed. How do you do that? You build trust, and then—as we discussed in chapter 8—you empower your employees:

- Define clear results for each employee.
- Make your employees accountable to results, not just constant activity.
- Provide the support and resources that they need to be successful.
- Establish the boundaries and level of authority for completing the task or project.

By providing a clear vision of the results you expect—rather than micro-managing each activity along the way—you communicate your *trust* in the employee's ability to do the job. This, again, is the essence of employee empowerment. However, managers who have experienced problems with "empowering" employees usually fare poorly in clearly defining the desired results, or in providing sufficient training. When failure occurs, the ineffective manager doesn't use the opportunity to evaluate the cause of failure; rather, the assumption is that the *employee* failed or, worse, the "empowerment" process was a failure.

Conclusion

What cannot be lost in this discussion is the critical necessity of having good people on your team to begin with. Frank Pacetta demonstrated in his experience with Xerox that substantial performance changes are often the result of how people are treated and how they are led. While high-performance teams begin first with capable, talented employees, it still takes a great manager to mine the potential of those employees.

In his groundbreaking best-seller, *Good to Great*, Jim Collins asserts that the key to creating "great" organizations is to get "the right people on the bus," an allusion to getting qualified and capable people on your team. Moreover, he emphatically states that, "People are *not* your most important assets. The *right* people are."[106]

Clearly, I am not suggesting that an environment of engagement will allow employees with below-average talent to outperform the competition. Simply put, good teams must have good players. However, I am emphatically stating that high performance is not possible—at least not for very long—in the wrong environment. Employees will slowly disengage as managers fail to acknowledge and value their contribution to the company.

Creating a high-performance work environment requires talented employees *and* a talented manager, but creating an environment of *engagement* is the responsibility of the team *leader*—the manager.

Creating an Environment of Employee Engagement

1-on-1 Insights™

- Managers complain loudly when their employees won't take responsibility for their actions, but when performance or productivity declines, the same managers will automatically blame their employees and fail to look at themselves.

- Recognition and encouragement are vital to employee satisfaction and engagement—and they don't cost a dime.

- Make sure your employees can do the basics of the job well. Never assume they know how—make sure.

- Remember: what gets *inspected* gets done. If you tell your employees one thing is important, and inspect (or measure or reward) something else, they will do what gets inspected.

- When basic human needs are fulfilled in the workplace—the need for trust, the need to have hope, the need to feel a sense of worth, and the need to feel competent—employees remain connected, engaged, and interested in pursuing the objectives of the company.

10
The 1-on-1 Meeting™

Developing employee potential requires individual attention

"The only managerial activities worthy of the name are one-on-one; everything else is window dressing."

—David Maister

In 1996, Joe Torre assumed the reins of the most storied sports franchise in American history, the New York Yankees. Unfortunately for Torre, New Yorkers were underwhelmed at the time. The *New York Post* announced his arrival with this headline: "Clueless Joe Torre."[107]

After nineteen years of managing the Mets, Braves, and Cardinals, Torre's record was a less-than-inspiring 894 wins and 1,003 losses, with only one play-off appearance (Braves, 1982). Compounding the problem for Yankee fans, the Bronx Bombers hadn't celebrated an AL Pennant since 1981—the longest such streak in Yankee history. To clear-thinking baseball fans, hiring Torre was a blunder of significant proportions—unless, of course, you hated the Yankees.

1-on-1 Management

However, Torre wasted little time in silencing the skeptics. In his first season, the Yankees cruised to 92 wins, captured the AL pennant and triumphed in the World Series, besting the Atlanta Braves in six games. Over the course of the next seven years, Torre and the Yankees returned to the October Classic five more times and, in three of those outings, emerged the winner.

Four World Series championships in eight years. Not too bad for "Clueless Joe."

Some observers would suggest that a wealth of talent and Major League Baseball's highest payroll were the determining factors in Torre's success with the Yankees. One *Fortune* magazine article viewed it quite differently:

> Consider: For five seasons he has taken a collection of rookies and retreads, recovering drug addicts and born-again Christians, Cuban defectors and defective throwers, and created a workplace that, were it not for its particular job requirements, would surely qualify for FORTUNE's list of the 100 best places to work. He has managed up as well as down, taming a notorious boss while buffering his players from the worst of the New York media maelstrom.[108]

Undoubtedly, talent is critical to any organization's success, but Torre's management style had plenty to do with returning the Yanks to their former glory. His approach to dealing with players includes a cornerstone of 1-on-1 Management™— consistent, one-on-one meetings:

The 1-on-1 Meeting™

Baseball legend Gene Mauch once said that it's easier for 25 players to understand one manager than for one manager to understand 25 players. Torre operates under the opposite premise. He sets a few basic rules (don't be late, no excessive facial hair, no loud music in the clubhouse), but that's it for across-the-board edicts. His principal management tool is not the big team meeting—he has little use for generic motivational talks—but *regular one-on-one encounters* [italics mine] with his players, which he uses to both monitor and regulate their psyches.[109]

The 1-on-1 Meeting™

At the heart of 1-on-1 Management™ is a consistent and planned meeting with those employees that report to you directly. Consistent means frequently and predictably; planned means that both employee and manager prepare beforehand. This meeting is designed to include only those employees that report directly to you, and over the years, I have found that weekly 1-on-1 Meetings™ work best. In some of my circumstances, less frequent meetings were used, but in general, a weekly get-together produced the best results and the most effective dialogue with employees.

One objection that may surface with regard to individual meetings is the challenge of dealing with a large number of employees. Undoubtedly, there are situations where managers have dozens of people reporting to them. In certain instances, and for good reason, this may be a standard practice, but in most situations, it is prudent to reduce the number of people

1-on-1 Management

reporting to you directly, if possible. For example, while you may be responsible for managing a department of thirty-six people, you might have two assistant managers and two supervisors, or something similar. In this scenario, you can easily establish 1-on-1 Meetings™ with each of the assistant managers and supervisors, and one of your primary objectives is to teach your managers/supervisors the principles of developing people through 1-on-1 Management™.

If you have more than six to eight people reporting to you directly, you may need to modify your meeting frequency to accommodate the number of people; however, there *is* no substitute for 1-on-1 Meetings™. Your people need your time and your attention. They need your encouragement and support. They need to have their performance assessed more frequently than once a year. They need consistent feedback and coaching because employee development and growth is critical to employee engagement.

If you are a front-line supervisor, for example, you would seek to meet weekly with the employees under your oversight. If you are a middle manager, you might meet with any combination of supervisors and/or individual employees—but only those reporting to you directly. If you are a senior manager or executive, you would meet with the managers that report to you directly.

To be clear, the 1-on-1 Meeting™ is not the usual "one-to-many" meeting typical of the corporate workplace; instead, it is specifically designed to provide a manager with the opportunity to review performance, set priorities, discuss needs for ongoing projects, and communicate about corporate and personal issues as needed. These short meetings—generally thirty to forty-five

The 1-on-1 Meeting™

minutes in duration—allow managers to maintain a consistent dialogue with direct reports.

I am also not suggesting that the traditional corporate meeting will be eliminated; indeed, they are likely a necessary part of management. Staff meetings, for example, have a variety of objectives, all of them important:

- Task assignment and/or coordination.
- Budget preparation and/or review.
- Brainstorming.
- Training and development.
- Project management.

1-on-1 Meetings™, however, are quite different—they are designed primarily to foster a personal and direct dialogue with the employee. When these meetings are consistent and well-executed, they contribute significantly to creating an environment of engagement. Arguably, one of the most significant challenges faced by managers in today's business climate is identifying and hiring talent; the corollary to that challenge—as we discussed in chapter 9—is the difficulty of keeping that talent on-board!

The Impact of 1-on-1 Meetings™

In addition to the excellent example provided by Joe Torre's management approach, we have discussed two other perfect examples of leaders who have used one-on-one meetings with dramatic results: Commander Abrashoff in the Navy, and Elzbieta Górska-Kolodziejczyk at International Paper in Poland.

1-on-1 Management

On the day that Commander Abrashoff assumed command of the USS *Benfold*, he recognized that traditional command-and-control management techniques would inevitably lead to substandard performance and further discontent from his crew. Recognizing the challenge before him, his first order of business was to "treat every encounter with every person on the ship as the most important thing in my world at that moment."[110] It is critical to note that Abrashoff's meetings with individual sailors were much different than what the typical manager might imagine. The meeting wasn't designed to tell the sailor what to do or to threaten dire consequences if things didn't change. Quite the contrary. It was specifically designed to elicit feedback that would lead to an improved understanding of the individual and to gather ideas of how to improve the work environment:

> I met individually with every sailor on the Benfold and asked each the same set of questions: Where are you from? Why did you join the navy? What's your family situation? Is there anything the navy can do to help your family? What do you like most about the Benfold? What do you like least? What would you change if you could?[111]

Although she managed far fewer employees, Górska-Kolodziejczyk's approach at International Paper was strikingly similar:

> To help her better manage the team, Górska began meeting individually with her workers. "I started with listening

to them, what they have to say, how they see it, how they would want the work to be organized, what more would they expect, what kind of work materials are they lacking," she says. "At the same time, I wrote down their problems and issues they wanted to be resolved. When we met again, I reported on what had been done. It also brought us closer."[112]

Clearly, individual meetings with employees are incredibly powerful. Great managers realize that creating high performance is substantially contingent on developing a relationship of trust with each employee. It is 1-on-1 Meetings™ that provide the means and opportunity to connect directly with each employee, to develop a coaching and mentoring relationship, to provide consistent feedback on performance, and to communicate more effectively.

With these benefits in mind, it would be a serious mistake to underestimate the value of 1-on-1 Meetings™. At the same time, it would also be a serious mistake to underestimate the time and energy required to do them properly!

First, it is a far different approach to management. It focuses on leadership and developing people rather than issuing orders and answering questions. Managers are usually far more comfortable completing typical managerial tasks—answering questions, solving problems, assigning work, completing reports, and so forth. Unfortunately, these things do little to develop, empower, and engage employees.

Second, it changes the time management priorities for a manager—individual 1-on-1 Meetings™ take time, something most managers scream that they don't have any to spare.

Third, it requires skills that many managers have not yet acquired. It takes time and training to learn how to communicate well or how to coach and mentor effectively.

Although 1-on-1 Management™ requires a change in a manager's perspective, these changes produce results—often dramatic results! Commander Abrashoff, for example, saved the navy millions of dollars in recruiting and training costs while improving the ship's combat readiness to best-in-fleet. At International Paper, Górska-Kolodziejczyk, the company's lone female manager, completely reversed the fortunes of a department that three previous managers—all men—had failed to energize. Her efforts vaulted employee engagement in the department from the bottom 25 percent of the company to the top 25 percent in only two years.

Such is the power of individual attention.

Your First 1-on-1 Meeting™

As you will see, the 1-on-1 Meeting™ is very simple, structurally. The success of these meetings is dependent on your ability to ask good questions, listen closely to the answers, and develop a relationship of trust that creates effective feedback. You should already have begun to work on communicating your performance expectations clearly (chapter 6). You should also be well on your way to addressing the four critical questions that all employees ask (chapters 7 & 8). If so, you have likely begun to create a stir among your department or team. Your employees are almost certainly beginning to notice something different about your management style.

The 1-on-1 Meeting™

As you implement 1-on-1 Meetings™, take care to proceed slowly at first and make sure each employee understands exactly what your intentions are. In fact, you should expect some initial skepticism if your employees are not accustomed to one-on-one encounters with the boss. They may even ask you outright if they are in some kind of trouble. Reassure each employee that your motives are very specific and transparent.

Here is an approach you might use to introduce your first 1-on-1 Meeting™:

> *"My objective is to be as effective as possible as a manager. I think people tend to enjoy their jobs more when they know the company cares about them and they have a chance to reach their goals. I need to change some of the things I do to make that happen, and I want to start by learning a lot more about the people that work for me."*

Indeed, the first meeting is designed to do nothing more than open up a dialogue and enable you to learn much more about each employee and his or her view of the company. While subsequent meetings will incorporate a very specific 1-on-1 Meeting™ template, this first meeting will be limited to asking a specific set of questions that enable you to gain a greater understanding of the employees' goals and perspectives:

1. What do you like about your job?

2. What do you dislike about your job? What part of your job creates the most problems for you?

3. Given the opportunity, what would you change about your job? Why?

1-on-1 Management

4. Where would you like to see your career go?

5. What can I do to help you reach your objectives?

These five questions will allow you to learn more about what motivates your employees, and also provide the opportunity for those employees to provide input on the jobs they do, the direction of their careers, any changes that could be made, and the support they may need.

A word of caution is required here. This meeting cannot be conducted in some sort of mechanical fashion in which you do not truly engage the employee and seek to understand his or her perspectives. In my experience, people easily discern the motivations of others, and you must prepare yourself to fully listen and consider the information that you obtain. If employees perceive this process as nothing more than the management "flavor-of-the-month," you will not only fail to connect with them, but you will also most likely reinforce any negative impressions they may have of you or the company.

True, it may not be feasible to act on all of the changes they suggest, but you must decide to be open-minded to any proposed changes and be fully capable of justifying your responses should they be rejected. The wrong thing to do is to reject an idea immediately simply because things have never been done that way before, or because it would require substantial effort to implement, or worst of all, because it wasn't your idea!

Take the time to evaluate each and every idea on its merits, and consider the potential impact on the performance of your team or the company. Put some stock in your employees' input—they are on the firing line every day, and often know what works and what doesn't.

1-on-1 Meeting™ Agenda

Now let's look at the typical, weekly 1-on-1 Meeting™. The first thing to understand prior to each 1-on-1 Meeting™ is that these meetings will not be nearly as effective if you dominate the conversation! The most effective approach is to ask good questions and then listen intently; a good rule-of-thumb is to be listening about 75 percent of the time. For many managers, this means resisting the temptation to fix every issue that arises, which may be completely contrary to your nature. In fact, if you are widely recognized as a knowledge expert, technical wizard, or problem-solver extraordinaire, your biggest struggle in this process may be to simply sit and listen.

This is not to suggest that you won't be offering advice or direction at certain points along the way, but your objective is to create a *dialogue* that allows your employees to contribute their ideas, assess their own work performance, and feel "in" on things (remember chapter 3?).

The second critical idea for these meetings is that they are for the employee's benefit even more so than yours. When I did these meetings with my employees, I would tell them, "This is your meeting." I designed the structure of the meeting to allow employees to talk out issues, provide feedback on problems they encountered, and determine what resources I could provide to help them achieve success. It was my opportunity to encourage them to think critically, while providing direct access to my input when needed.

Here is the format I have followed in 1-on-1 Meetings™:

1-on-1 Management

1. Review—discuss key events of the previous week.

2. Preview—outline significant events for the upcoming week.

3. Plan—establish expectations, discuss resources needed.

4. Prioritize—establish critical goals/objectives to be advanced or completed.

That's it. Simple, straightforward, and to the point. Once an employee has been through this process a few times, he or she will automatically begin to prepare for the meetings using this approach. [Note: If you would like a form designed specifically to be used in the 1-on-1 Meeting™, you can download one free at www.1-on-1Management.com.]

This process keeps you, the manager, completely up-to-speed on the progress of critical processes and projects. Simply by discussing those items, you make the employee accountable for progress and completion. When challenges arise, they hit your radar almost immediately, which prevents problems from being avoided or hidden from your attention. Finally, these conversations give you excellent opportunities to coach, encourage, and create trust.

For the employee, these weekly conversations provide the opportunity to meet and communicate directly with the boss. It is impossible to overestimate the impact these meetings have on the employee if the dialogue is open and frank. At the same time, the manager has a very good idea of the level of engagement of each employee.

The 1-on-1 Meeting™

Part 1: Review

As you begin your meeting, ask questions designed to update the key objectives the employee accomplished in the previous week. A quick and easy way to start is to say, "Tell me about last week—what key things did you accomplish?" You may find that employees are prone to getting bogged down in too much detail, so encourage them to give you the highlights from the past week and reserve discussions regarding details until the end. This provides a summary or overview of the previous week in just a few minutes, leaving you with a good understanding of progress and direction.

There are situations where you will want to pursue more details. For instance, if the employee describes a problem or challenge that occurred, dig into the details and prompt them to describe how they dealt with the situation. One of the objectives of 1-on-1 Management™ is to encourage critical thinking, and this process will help you to understand how the employee thinks and solves problems, and will also provide the opportunity to coach them in key situations (more on this in chapter 11).

Another opportunity to dig into additional details might be if the employee describes a key project or assignment that has been completed, or a task that has furthered the company's key values or objectives. This may provide a perfect opportunity for you to recognize or praise the result, either in the 1-on-1 Meeting™ or at a later time when you can do it publicly.

Finally, there may be times when you suspect that your employee are glossing over potential problems or even embellishing their role in an accomplishment. This is the time to ask questions to elicit more details in order to discover the true nature of these circumstances. It is not uncommon for marginal performers to attempt to overstate their contributions or avoid discussing areas where they have not met your expectations. Drill down with more questions to uncover these issues, but, as a great manager, do not become accusatory or sarcastic in the process.

When a manager discusses an employee's shortcomings or failures, it is critical to remain even-tempered and focused on the behavior, not the employee. Anger, sarcasm, or accusations will only serve to deteriorate an already sensitive discussion, and, inevitably, will lead to more problems instead of solutions and changes in behavior.

There is a significant upside to the 1-on-1 Meetings™: sub-par performance or negative attitudes will be identified more quickly, and can be addressed much sooner, than in the traditional annual performance review.

Part 2: Preview

After a review of the previous week's activity, the next logical step is to talk about the upcoming week and the objectives that need to be addressed. Ask the employee to outline his or her key activities for the week, and take this opportunity to interject any new projects or tasks that need to be added to the workload.

It should be obvious to you that the objectives set for the coming week become those items that will probably be reviewed in next week's meeting. This provides dual benefits to the manager and the employee: continuity from one meeting to the next and an "automatic" accountability process as you establish expectations for the week.

A great manager will establish an expectation for *results* rather than micro-managing the details of the process. The exception to this idea occurs when the employee is being trained to do something new or unfamiliar, and you are required to train them in a specific process or skill. If, however, the employee has the skills and resources to complete a task or project, it is a simple matter of outlining the results that you desire. Once you have established your expectation of those results, it is important to use the *Review* portion of subsequent 1-on-1 Meetings™ to analyze the critical thinking skills of the employee as a completed project or task is desribed. This will inevitably lead to additional opportunities to train and/or coach.

Part 3: Plan and Prioritize

As you discuss the upcoming week's activities and objectives, allow the employee to prioritize the importance and sequence of each. Rather than dictating your own priorities, encourage the employee to define the critical "next steps" of each project or task, prioritize their completion, and establish the short- and long-term timelines. If you are not necessarily in agreement with any of those items, ask questions that allow them to explain their reasoning.

As you ask questions, most employees will assume that you may not agree with their plans or priorities, so suggest to them that talking out the decision-making process demonstrates to you how they think and helps to clarify the decisions reached.

1-on-1 Management

Of course, there will plenty of times when your input and direction will be required, but resist the need to make every decision, dictate every detail, and determine each step in the work.

A significant part of the 1-on-1 Meeting™ is creating a work environment that allows employees to develop their own skills so that your effectiveness is multiplied. Many managers become the choke point or bottleneck in the work flow of a company simply because nothing can be done without their directive or approval. This not only limits productivity, but also stifles creativity and leads directly to employee disengagement.

The last item of importance in planning is to identify and acquire any resources the employee may need to complete any of the agreed upon objectives. He or she may need access to equipment or data not readily available, personnel or materials from other departments, or support from you or other employees. Whatever the need, it is important to make sure that the employee has the necessary resources, as needed, to accomplish the objectives set during the meeting.

When you have completed the 1-on-1 Meeting™, you will have worked together to establish clear objectives with appropriate timelines, and you should have removed any barriers that might prevent success. You will have communicated quite clearly your expectations for performance and empowered the employee to produce results, with the expectation that that next week's meeting will review those results.

One significant benefit to this approach is that performance issues are quickly identified and, quite often, will be addressed and overcome long before the traditional "annual review" process would even identify the problem. Further, when the employee has a significant role in the planning process—setting objectives, defining next steps, establishing priorities—the manager is adding yet another dimension of creating a powerful environment of engagement.

Feedback and Dialogue

Although feedback is not identified as a "step" in the 1-on-1 Meeting™ template, it is nonetheless a guiding principle in the 1-on-1 Management™ process. As Ken Blanchard has noted, "Feedback is the breakfast of champions."[113] However, the challenge for managers is to provide feedback in such a way that employees are motivated to change direction or change behavior in a positive and enthusiastic way.

Constructive feedback may be a simple suggestion, an idea, or an observation, but feedback that results in changes in direction or behavior is likely to arise from an ongoing dialogue fostered by the manager. This type of feedback is usually not a direct criticism of performance but a discovery process that is guided by a series of questions.

We will take an in-depth look at feedback and dialogue, and other elements of the coaching process, in chapter 11.

Conclusion

The 1-on-1 Meeting™ is a simple, yet powerful, method to improve communication with your employees, and it is a dramatic improvement over the traditional performance review process since you are discussing expectations of job performance on a weekly basis. These meetings also allow you to consistently address the two primary needs that employees

1-on-1 Management

have: the need to be appreciated for their contributions and the need to have the opportunity to be in on things.

The great manager uses these meetings to guide, to coach, to establish expectations, to correct when necessary, to empower, and to communicate in ways that are simply not possible in one-to-many meetings or e-mail messages.

At this point, we can see how effective communication is the driving force in the Management Leadership Cycle™:

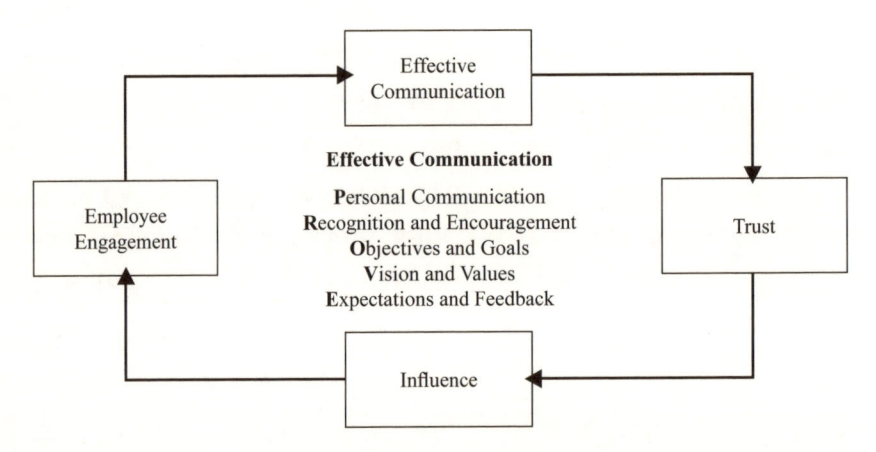

Effective Communication
Personal Communication
Recognition and Encouragement
Objectives and Goals
Vision and Values
Expectations and Feedback

Fig. 1: Management Leadership Cycle™

Management leadership is a flywheel that gains momentum as the quantity and quality of communication increases. Effective communication—through words or actions—is directly or indirectly tied to the factors that create trust. As a manager develops trust, the ability and opportunity to positively influence employees increases commensurately, and as we have discovered, leadership is influence. It is this leadership that engages employees. *Remember, leadership defines an organization.*

The 1-on-1 Meeting™

What, then, is the primary driver of employee engagement? Without question, it is effective communication. Further, as employees become more and more engaged in the workplace, the quality of the communication—and the relationship with the manager—continues to improve.

The final piece of the puzzle is to develop and use a feedback loop in the communication process to coach and develop each employee. Great managers look beyond even performance improvements and team development; the great manager's ultimate objective is to help every employee develop their potential and reach their own personal goals and career objectives.

1-on-1 Insights™

- Great managers use one-on-one meetings with their employees. It is the best way—perhaps the only effective way—to communicate, review job performance, establish expectations, and create trust.

- Nobody has a better idea of what is wrong with the company, or what the company could be doing better, than the employees on the front line. Ask them how the company or team might improve, and listen carefully to what they have to say.

- Engaged employees save the company a tremendous amount of money: their performance is better, their attitudes are better, and they stay with the company instead of leaving for a better manager. The cost savings in reducing employee turnover alone are enormous.

Coaching in the Workplace

Great coaches manage well; great managers coach well

> "The growth and development of people is the highest calling of leadership."
>
> —Harvey S. Firestone

In 1980, Michael William Krzyzewski accepted the position of head basketball coach at Duke University in Durham, North Carolina. Coach K, as he is universally referred to now, began his coaching career at Army, leading the Cadets to seventy-three wins and two National Invitational Tournament (NIT) berths in five years.

His first 3 years at Duke did little to foreshadow what would become one of the great college basketball dynasties of all time. After a 17-13 record and an NIT tournament invitation in his first season, Krzyzewski suffered through two consecutive losing seasons and accumulated a rather unimpressive 38-47 record. A season-ending, 43-point loss to Virginia in 1983 marked the low point for Coach K:

1-on-1 Management

I remember that night we went to a small restaurant, more like a fast-food place. And (I remember) a bunch of people around, drinking some iced tea and sodas, and somebody said, 'Well here's to forgetting about tonight.' And I said, 'No no, here's to never forgetting about tonight. Because this is a reference point. In order to appreciate where we're going to be, we have to know how this felt, how losing felt.'[114]

The turnaround began the following season as Duke improved to 24-10 and Coach K earned his first trip to the NCAA post-season tournament. A rite of passage, the NCAA tournament—known as the "Big Dance"—is the yardstick by which college basketball success is measured. Indeed, as many coaches have observed, just getting into the tournament is the ultimate objective of every NCAA basketball team:

". . . there are 260 other teams who would love to be here playing in this game. If you ask them if they'd like to be in the NCAA Tournament tomorrow night or watching it on TV, I guarantee you they'd be here. It's a wonderful experience for us, and for our kids. It's a once in a lifetime experience and I hope it can continue."[115]

It certainly continued for Coach K, who has returned to the NCAA tournament every year he has coached except one, an astounding twenty-three times in twenty-four years.[116] And Duke's performance in the tournament has been nothing short of spectacular: ten Final Four appearances, three national

Coaching in the Workplace

championships, and sixty-eight NCAA tournament victories—an NCAA record. In fact, only three other coaches have won three or more NCAA basketball titles in the history of Division I college basketball.[117]

Throughout his tenure, the Blue Devils have piled up wins at an amazing clip—664 victories since 1983, almost 28 wins every year for 24 years![118] In 2001, Coach K's spectacular success prompted *Time* magazine and CNN to honor him as "America's Best Coach."[119] While wins and losses were most certainly a determining factor in the choice, players and team observers believe that Coach K's success is as much about management and leadership as it is about X's and O's:

> "The way he can connect with everybody, it's unbelievable," says Brad Miller, Team USA big man (at 7 ft.), who plays for the Sacramento Kings. "I'd have our [NBA] team pay him a couple of grand to talk to us."

He'd have to up the ante—Krzyzewski commands up to $100,000 a speech, and his name even graces an academic arm, the Fuqua/Coach K Center of Leadership & Ethics at Duke. All this for a guy who teaches men in shorts how to toss balls through a hoop. "He talks about character issues that are soulful," says Morgan Stanley CEO John Mack, whose managing directors—"a pretty cynical group," he notes—raved about a recent Krzyzewski talk. "It's about honesty, it's about love, and often times, in the big world, you don't see many leaders get up and talk about things like that." Mack equates Krzyzewski's leadership skills to those of legends like IBM's Lou Gerstner and GE's Jack Welch [italics mine].120

1-on-1 Management

Learning Management from Coaches

Successful coaches like Krzyzewski provide a perfect example of what corporate managers might accomplish if they approached their jobs as an exercise in developing people the way coaches do. A close inspection reveals that athletic coaches are required to plan, organize, lead, and control just like their corporate counterparts, and like many corporate managers, they are responsible for producing a product that consumers "buy." While failure for an athletic coach is usually measured in wins and losses, the results of failure on the field (or floor) are also calculated financially. A winning team translates into increased ticket sales, concession revenue, corporate sponsorships, and sales of team memorabilia.

Coaches, in other words, are simply managers—managers who are *forced* to teach and improve the performance of their players because the players are the product. However, even Coach K admits that coaches often miss the connection between success and people:

> "A common mistake among those who work in sports is spending a disproportional amount of time on X's and O's as compared to time spent learning about people."[121]

It's not that Coach K would deny the importance of "X's and O's;" but to produce a championship caliber team, coaches are required to coordinate the performance of several individuals into successful *team* play. Learning about those players, from Coach K's perspective, is just as important as the skills

Coaching in the Workplace

and strategies employed in the game. The talents of each player must be carefully matched to the right position, while basic skills must be developed and improved to their full potential. Then, the actions of five different players at any one time must be carefully coordinated—and practiced to perfection—to produce a winning basketball team.

The same process is true in the workplace. A skillful manager must carefully match individual job requirements to the skills and potential of the employee, and then provide the training necessary to fully develop that potential. At the same time, the efforts of individual team members must be *coordinated*. Too few managers understand the vast importance of creating a team—a group of employees that work in concert with one another to reach a clear and elevating goal (chapter 7).

Back to basketball: careful observation of a basketball practice reveals that coaches follow a predictable approach to team development; *successful team execution is preceded by the improvement of individual skills.* Practices typically begin with the team divided into smaller groups, and drills are used to teach individual (one-on-one) skills: dribbling, passing, shooting, rebounding, free throws, and so on. Then, players are assembled to practice and coordinate different phases of the game: offensive tactics, fast breaks, transition defense, or in-bounds plays, for example. Finally, the entire team will gather to scrimmage and simulate game conditions, allowing the coach to observe and teach "team" mechanics.

To summarize, team development begins with the teaching of individual skills, progresses to sub-groups that work together on phases of the game, and then advances to "team" practice that coordinates the play of each player on the team.

1-on-1 Management

1-on-1 Principle™: Team success is a function of the development and coordination of individual players.

However, while individual skills improvement is critical to team success, Duke's Coach K believes that learning about people is more than just creating better players; it is about creating an environment where the sum of the collective players is greater than their individual parts:

> I think first of all, it can't be "my team." It has to be "our team." Where we create an environment where the players are not playing for me; they're playing for us. And when you establish that, you establish ownership for everybody on the team and you play as one. That was the biggest thing about this season (1999-2000). The team was better together than the total amount of what the individuals could do.[122]

Great managers, like great coaches, understand that high-performance teams are *necessarily* composed of high-performance individuals. Great corporate managers, like their successful counterparts in athletics, seek out great players to add to the team, but approach the process of *team* development by developing the individual skills of each employee. Then, those individual employees are coached to coordinate their individual skills into a high-performance work unit.

——————— Coaching in the Workplace ———————

The Impact of Coaching

In athletics, it is not at all uncommon for a good coach to have an enormous impact on a team's performance and in many instances, a good coach provides inspiration and motivation to an individual player. In the same way, the corporate *manager* who thinks and manages like a coach can have exactly the same impact on a company and an individual employee. As it turns out, coaching on the field and coaching in the office have similar objectives and comparable results, as discussed in the book *Primal Leadership: Learning to Lead with Emotional Intelligence:*

> "Coaching's surprisingly positive emotional impact stems largely from the empathy and rapport a leader establishes with employees. A good [corporate] coach communicates a belief in people's potentials and an expectation that they can do their best."[123]

Coaching, in athletics or in the workplace, will often have a dramatic impact on a player or an employee because good coaches develop a strong rapport with the individual and encourage—even demand—performance excellence. In clichéd terms, great coaches believe in us, perhaps even when we don't believe in ourselves. I personally experienced the influence of a great coach when I played high school football in the late '70s. The difference maker was a man named Larry Coker, a successful coach who already had a pair of state titles under his belt when he became our head football coach my senior year.

1-on-1 Management

His impact was immediate; after only six wins the previous two years combined, we rolled to an 11-2 season and a trip to the state semi-finals.

Coker would later move into the collegiate ranks, serving as the Offensive Coordinator at the University of Tulsa, Oklahoma State University, and the University of Oklahoma. Following a stint at Ohio State, he joined the staff at the University of Miami in 1995 and then became the head coach in 2001. In his first year, Coker led the Hurricanes to a perfect 14-0 season and an NCAA national championship, and the 'Canes narrowly missed a second consecutive title in 2002 following a controversial double-overtime loss to Ohio State, 31-24. In both seasons, Coker was recognized as the Big East Coach of the Year and the National Coach of the Year.[124]

Like all successful coaches, Coker was a sound technician—good with X's and O's—but his primary objective when he arrived in the small town of Claremore, Oklahoma, was to give us a reason to believe in ourselves again. Losing creates doubt and destroys confidence, and after two years of failure, winning was neither a habit nor an expectation. Coker's approach to this problem was simple, yet effective: teach each player to pay attention to the details and stress improvement each and every week. Do those things, he said, and the wins will take care of themselves.

Coker wasn't a "rah-rah" coach or a big speech maker, but he had two enormous talents that are critical for developing winning teams. First of all, he was a great teacher. A close friend of mine told me years later that he learned more about the game of football in that one year during high school than in all of his previous years of experience. Coker helped each player improve his individual skills, and then taught us how those skills connected to on-field team performance. Practice made more sense. Individual players better understood their impact on the team and their contribution to the success of each play.

Secondly, Coker developed extraordinary trust in his players. His words and his actions created trust; he was genuine and sincere and took an interest in each player. In an era when a team prayer prior to each game was commonplace, he always led our team in prayer and finished with this thought: "And thank you for allowing me to be their football coach." I never doubted for a moment that he meant every single word.

It didn't take long for his coaching philosophies to be tested; we lost our first game of the season and I played an especially critical part in the loss. Early in the game, I made a mistake in pass coverage and gave up a big play that cost us a touchdown. As hard as I was on myself, I expected much worse from the coaches at Monday's practice. However, Coker's response couldn't have surprised me more. He was positive, even optimistic, about the game's results. He pointed out that our mistakes were correctable, and he congratulated us on playing hard. Most importantly, he told us that we were going to win a lot of games that season. And we did.

Coaching in the Workplace

There is much that a corporate manager can learn from great coaches. Here are the key points to take away from the example of Larry Coker:

1-on-1 Management

- Make sure each employee can perform his or her job well, all the way down to the basic details. When employees are good at what they do, they develop confidence in their abilities.

- Train constantly and stress improvement. At the same time, don't become known as a manager that is never satisfied—recognize and encourage in direct proportion to achievement.

- Connect each employee's job output to the overall objectives of the company. As we have discussed, this gives the employee purpose and clearly establishes their importance to the team.

- Practice the habits that create trust. Be genuine. Develop a sincere interest in the welfare of your employees. Communicate effectively.

- When employees make mistakes, use the opportunity to coach and learn. Ultimately, this is what managers are supposed to do—develop employees.

The corporate world is replete with examples of managers at every level who have used the principles of coaching to develop winning teams. A case in point is Jack Welch. In 1981, he became General Electric's youngest chairman and CEO. At the age of forty-five, he replaced outgoing CEO Reginald H. "Reg" Jones, who ended his forty-two-year career on top of the business world. Jones' legacy included recognition as "the most admired business leader in America" and "the most influential person in business," and he was recognized as the CEO of the Year by Gallup.[125] Jones also left the proverbial cupboard full—GE had completed its twenty-sixth consecutive

Coaching in the Workplace

quarter of increased earnings with annual revenues in excess of $26.8 billion.

However, when Welch stepped down after twenty years as CEO, GE sales had multiplied over five times to a staggering $146 billion. The market value of the company had increased from $14 billion to well over $400 billion in 2004, making it the largest company in the world at that time. In 1999, Welch was recognized as the "Manager of the Century" by *Fortune* magazine.[126]

Like Coach K, Welch also recognizes the importance of coaching and developing people, as he outlines in his book, *Winning*:

> The team with the best players usually does win. And that is why, very simply, you need to invest the vast majority of your time and energy as a leader in three activities. You have to evaluate—making sure the right people are in the right jobs, supporting and advancing those who are, and moving out those who are not. You have to coach—guiding, critiquing and helping people to improve their performance in every way. And finally, you have to build self-confidence—pouring out encouragement, caring and recognition. Self-confidence energizes, and it gives your people the courage to stretch, take risks and achieve beyond their dreams. It is the fuel of winning teams.[127]

Evaluate. Coach. Build self-confidence. This is the "fuel" that drives winning teams. Welch not only believes in the value of coaching, but he was also willing to make a significant investment in training his company's leaders to coach. According to the company's Annual Report, GE invested $1 billion in training in 2001 alone, developing leaders who "spend much of their time coaching, developing, evaluating and mentoring great people inside the most rigorous talent development process in industry."[128]

Unfortunately, too few managers understand the need for individual coaching. One of the truly vivid examples of the difference between athletic coaches and corporate managers is the annual "performance review" process, a staple in the corporate workplace but completely unknown to professional athletes. Imagine the impact on the performance of an NBA basketball team if the coach approached the review process like many corporations do: "Alright, this season we're going to play 82 games, and at the end of the year, we will review your performance and tell you what you can do to improve your play next year."

There is very little chance you will ever hear that conversation in professional sports. Since a coach's job is dependent on the ability to win games, make the play-offs, and help the organization turn a substantial profit, game-to-game improvements are critical to success. This is exactly why high-performance athletes competing at the highest level of their profession practice several times weekly and receive consistent coaching to improve every part of their game.

Why should the workplace be any different?

What is "Coaching" in the Workplace?

What does it mean for a manager to "coach" in the workplace? Primarily, it means to approach the job of managing

Coaching in the Workplace

people from the perspective of developing talent—working with employees to help them identify their strengths, improve their skills, and provide the resources that enable them to be successful. From a 1-on-1 Management™ perspective then, coaching is defined as follows:

1. Communicating performance expectations.

2. Supporting and enabling performance improvement through ongoing training and skills development.

3. Providing ongoing assessment and feedback.

We have discussed the power of expectations in chapter 6, and the enormous benefits that employees derive from a clear understanding of them. Once your expectations are in place, the next logical step is for you to provide the training and support necessary for employees to meet those expectations, and then to consistently assess that performance and provide effective feedback that will allow employees to reach their goals.

Marshall Goldsmith, recognized by the American Management Association as one of fifty great thinkers and business leaders impacting the field of management over the past eighty years,[129] is widely regarded as a leading authority in helping leaders affect positive and lasting change in behavior through coaching. In 2000, along with Laurence Lyons and Alyssa Freas, Goldsmith edited and contributed to a landmark book on coaching entitled *Coaching for Leadership*. In the book's first article, Lyons says this about coaching in the workplace:

> With a sound appreciation of business and interpersonal dynamics, a good coach is simply a process person who can establish rapport; is informed about the . . . immediate

environment; is honest and courageous in providing feedback; is a good listener; asks good questions; is visionary and analytical; and is a good planner who seeks follow-up and closure.[130]

First and foremost, a good coach is someone who can "establish rapport;" in fact, it is nearly impossible to provide meaningful coaching to someone with whom you haven't established a relationship of trust. As we have seen, establishing trust is a critical component in leadership—one that relies heavily on effective communication and one that does not happen overnight. However, as trust develops, the opportunity to impact performance improves dramatically. Feedback is not viewed as a personal attack, and a manager's actions are not perceived as being the result of a personal, selfish agenda.

It is, therefore, important to realize that it will be difficult to simply "jump in" and start coaching your employees if you have never done so. It will be especially difficult to coach if that rapport, or trust, has not yet been developed. Therefore, you should start at the beginning: begin to work on communicating effectively, begin to establish your expectations for performance, and begin to create an environment of engagement. Throughout these processes, solicit the input of your employees and listen carefully to their responses.

How to Coach Your Employees

Coaching is a skill that can be learned and developed; the only prerequisite is a sincere desire to help your employees reach their potential. While a manager should look at the improvement

Coaching in the Workplace

of his or her coaching skills as an ongoing and long-term process, it is easy to get started. You can learn the basics of coaching and have a positive impact on your employees—now.

In fact, if you have begun to use 1-on-1 Meetings™ as a management tool, you have created the opportunity and methodology to begin coaching your employees. While it is certainly possible to coach effectively without implementing 1-on-1 Meetings™, a consistent weekly meeting offers the means to provide ongoing assessment and feedback—the foundation of coaching.

Feedback is the one tool that provides the means for an athlete or an employee to improve performance, but when a manager fails to create rapport with an employee, feedback is often perceived as criticism. There are, in fact, managers who wield feedback—actually criticism—like a weapon, using it as a demonstration of power or authority. These managers often leap to criticize, thinking that a good manager's role is to correct an employee's behavior. The work environment created by these managers rarely provides adequate encouragement or recognition, and the ongoing criticism creates enormous resentment.

At the other end of the spectrum, there are other managers who simply dislike confrontation and avoid the use of feedback for fear of creating conflict with an employee. In *Coaching for Leadership*, Marshall Goldsmith makes the following observation regarding confrontation:

> Leaders are often afraid that confronting people about poor teamwork or other behavioral shortcomings (as opposed to performance problems) will cause them to be disliked. The

paradox is, leaders would be respected more, not less, for delivering the bad news.[131]

In either case, feedback itself is not the issue; it is the manager's perspective on feedback that leads to problems. One extreme (harsh criticism) leads to employee disengagement or turnover while the other extreme (avoidance) creates frustration, since managerial feedback is the only way that an employee is able to gain an understanding of why and how to improve performance.

Constructive feedback, then, is neither critical nor confrontational in the classic sense of the words. It is simply a process of discovery, which results from questions and good listening skills. As a manager/coach reviews performance, questions are used to draw out the details of outcomes:

- How are you doing on this project?
- Were you pleased with the results?
- What could have been done differently?
- When you completed the work, did you discover any areas for improvement?
- Who might have helped you achieve a better result?

Notice that there is one question that is not asked in the review process: "*Why?*"

- *Why* didn't you finish that report on time?
- *Why* do you consistently overlook details?
- *Why* does it take you so long?

Coaching in the Workplace

- *Why* can't you ever complete your work accurately?
- *Why* didn't you get this done?

Using the word "why" to begin a question creates an accusatory tone that, more often than not, puts an employee on the defensive. Regardless of how the "why" question is answered, it inevitably sounds like an excuse, no matter how true it may be.

Manager: "Why did you miss your deadline?"

Employee: "Hey, it wasn't my fault. The marketing department didn't even send the information I asked for until yesterday."

Manager: "When did you ask them for the information?"

Employee: "Last Friday."

Manager: "Last Friday? You've been working on this project for three weeks. Why didn't you ask for it sooner?"

Employee: "It's customer demographic information, and I didn't even realize I needed it until I started work on the market segmentation section last week."

Manager: "Well, don't you think you should've thought that through a little more carefully?"

Employee: (Visibly annoyed) "Hey, this is a big project, and I only missed the deadline by two days. I can't help it if marketing takes forever to get information to us."

Manager: (Getting irritated) "Hey, don't get snippy with me—you're the one that missed the deadline. If you can't get these things done on time, we may need to make some changes."

1-on-1 Management

As you can see, this exchange can easily deteriorate into further accusations that will create animosity between the manager and the employee. If the manager has little or no rapport established with the employee, this conversation certainly isn't likely to lead to developing that rapport. Let's look at an alternative approach that eliminates the question of "why":

Manager: "How did you feel about the results of this project?"

Employee: "Well, I had a few problems, but overall I think it went pretty well."

Manager: "What kind of problems?"

Employee: "The biggest problem was the marketing department. They didn't send over the information I needed until yesterday, so I wound up missing the deadline by two days."

Manager: "What might you have done differently in order to meet the deadline?"

Employee: "Well, I might have asked for the information sooner, but I'm not really sure how I would have figured that out earlier in the project."

Manager: "OK, I think I see your point. You didn't know you needed the information until late in the project, and by the time you asked for it, you were in a time crunch."

Employee: "Exactly."

Manager: "When you arrived at the point in the project where you figured out you needed that marketing information, what happened that made you realize you were going to need it?"

Employee: "Well, when I started working on the market segmentation for the new product release, it dawned on me that I was going to need some actual customer demographic information from marketing to support my conclusions."

Manager: "So, once you got started on that section of the project, you realized you needed the information?"

Employee: "Yes."

Manager: "Theoretically, if you could get to that particular point sooner, then you would probably make the request to the marketing department sooner, right?"

Employee: "Absolutely."

Manager: "Alright, well let's brainstorm this a little bit. You really need to excel at developing these projects to move ahead in your career, so we need to figure out how you can plan them more effectively. Do you have any ideas?"

Employee: "I guess one thing I could've done is let you help me. You could've taken a look at my project to see if I was missing anything . . ."

Manager: "That's a good point. There is certainly nothing wrong with getting help or outside opinions. On the other hand, if you had outlined your approach to the project in detail before you started, do you think you might have anticipated the need for the customer demographic data?"

Employee: "Well . . . I might have, but I usually just jump in and get started right away. I guess I probably don't spend enough time on planning."

Manager: "That makes sense. My thought is that we need to work on developing your project planning skills. You should make a few changes so you can avoid missing a deadline again."

Employee: "I agree."

Now we are beginning to make some progress. The employee's attitude is not defensive—especially if he or she has developed a rapport with the manager and is convinced that the constructive feedback will advance his/her career.

One thing you will notice is the pronounced difference in the time required between the two approaches. *Coaching is an investment in your employees,* and that investment requires time. It takes time to establish expectations; it takes time to ask questions and listen to the answers; it takes time to work through issues productively.

1-on-1 Principle™: Effective people management requires a significant change in how you invest your available time.

Coaching, then, is a process that requires both time and planning. Like any other process, it is one that can be learned and duplicated. And it is a process that will allow you to develop the potential in each of your employees. Rather than relying on your technical expertise to solve every problem, you will be able to multiply your effectiveness by preparing your employees to solve their own problems.

Here are five important keys to effective coaching:

1. The first step is to *establish expectations for individual performance*. When an employee knows exactly what results are expected, it is much easier to compare actual performance to those expectations and make adjustments as needed.

2. The next step is to *routinely review employee performance*, which you can do weekly if you implement the 1-on-1 Meeting™.

3. In order to provide effective feedback, *ask good questions and listen carefully*. As we discussed in chapter 5, this is the best way to improve employee communication, and coaching is essentially about communication.

4. As you compare results to expectations, help employees to *identify any issues or barriers that exist*, and then help them discover ways to overcome them. This is really the core of good coaching—helping an employee improve skills and job performance through training.

5. Like all good coaches, *reinforce success* at every opportunity. As you review performance, encourage and praise success in order to build your employee's confidence.

Conclusion

The similarities between athletic coaches and workplace managers are uncanny. It is little wonder that Coach K is as much in demand as a speaker at business conferences as he is at basketball camps. Preparing individuals to outperform the competition and win games is what coaches do for a living. It is important to note that the coach doesn't play the game; he or she prepares the players to compete and then *leads* them into the competition.

1-on-1 Management

Similarly, managers should learn to train and develop employees. When they are able to learn and apply coaching principles, managers not only transform their employees, but transform themselves in the process: managers become leaders. As legendary NFL coach Vince Lombardi observed:

> Leaders aren't born; they are made. And they are made just like anything else, through hard work. And that's the price we'll have to pay to achieve that goal, or any goal.[132]

1-on-1 Insights™

- What sets the great manager apart is the ability to see the capabilities of indiviual employees even when they cannot yet see it for themselves, and then to help them develop those capabilities to their greatest potential.

- Being good with the "X's and O's" is one part of being a great manager. Another equally important part is being good with people, which you can learn just as well as the X's and O's.

- Invest the time to develop your employees. As they begin to do the work you thought only you were qualified to do, you will have more time available.

The 1-on-1 Development Plan™

Success is a destination that requires a plan

"Our goals can only be reached through a vehicle of a plan, in which we must fervently believe, and upon which we must vigorously act. There is no other route to success."

—Pablo Picasso

In 1976, United Artists and MGM released a film called *Rocky*, written by and starring an unknown actor named Sylvester Stallone. Today, of course, there are six *Rocky* films, including the 2006 release entitled *Rocky Balboa*, which has already grossed more than $155 million worldwide.[133]

The first film is the story of Rocky Balboa, an unfocused fighter with a mediocre record and a lackluster opinion of himself. Not surprisingly, it takes an experienced coach, Mickey "Mick" Goldmill, to see in Rocky what he can't see for himself:

> "... you had the talent to become a good fighter, and instead of that, you became a leg-breaker for some cheap, second-rate loan shark."[134]

1-on-1 Management

But fate offers Rocky the chance of a lifetime. When a contender for the heavyweight title suffers an injury prior to a scheduled title bout, Apollo Creed offers the fight to Rocky. Rocky, the "Italian Stallion," is a Philadelphia native, where the fight will be held, and Creed senses the opportunity to gin up interest in an otherwise meaningless event.

It is Mick, of course, who provides the inspiration, the training, and the focus that transforms Rocky from a clumsy street fighter into a pretty good boxer. In the end, Rocky—completely out of his league as the story begins—takes the champ a full fifteen rounds and narrowly loses in a stunning split-decision. "Ain't gonna be no rematch" said a bruised and bloody Apollo Creed at the end of the fight. "Don't want one," replied the equally battered Rocky.[135]

Sure, *Rocky* is a fictional account of fighter Rocky Balboa, but there are nonetheless a number of useful illustrations in the movie for managers. First of all, great managers, like great coaches, recognize and unlock the potential in their employees. Second, they provide inspiration through various doses of encouragement, praise, and challenges. Third, they create focus through discipline, training, and frequent performance review. Perhaps most importantly, they design and plan training to improve and develop skills.

Mick knew that Rocky would need to make significant improvements in his footwork, stamina, and punching skills to compete with a world champion. So, he pieced together a training regimen that would accomplish those things and then he pushed Rocky to be what he had already envisioned that Rocky could be.

―――――― The 1-on-1 Development Plan™ ――――――

The 1-on-1 Development Plan™ is a tool that allows a manager to do the same thing in the workplace. It is a tool that approaches employee development as a planning exercise—identifying the core skills and key competencies that an employee should develop to further his or her career. Plus, it is a tool that is easily integrated into the 1-on-1 Meeting™ we discussed in chapter 10.

The Importance of Goals

Mark Price played high school basketball in Enid, Oklahoma, and went on to play college basketball at Georgia Tech. An All-ACC performer for four years, Price was acquired in 1986 by the Dallas Mavericks as the first pick in the second round of the draft, but was immediately traded to the Cleveland Cavaliers. In twelve seasons in the NBA, Price was regarded as one of the finest shooters to play the game.

In 1989, he became one of only five players to finish a season shooting better than 90 percent from the free throw line, 50 percent from the field, and 40 percent from the three-point line.[136] Price also distinguished himself as the most accurate free throw shooter in NBA history. In 722 games, he shot an amazing 90.39 percent from the charity stripe, making 2,135 of his 2,362 attempts.[137]

Despite Price's incredible accuracy (he missed an average of only nineteen free throws each season), *you*—or anyone else—could outshoot Price every day of the week, if we could convince him to wear a blindfold during the competition. With no sense of where the basket is, he would have absolutely no chance to defeat you.

1-on-1 Management

The point is obvious. *Without goals, something to focus on and shoot for, none of us will be as successful as we might be.* But why does this fact seem to so easily escape the manager in the workplace? How can a manager or an employee strive for something that is not even defined? I have always loved this quote about goal-setting:

> In the absence of clearly-defined goals, we become strangely loyal to performing daily trivia until ultimately we become enslaved by it.[138]

In other words, without clear objectives, we can be easily distracted to work on things that may not contribute to our success. In chapter 7, we learned that a common element of successful teams is a clear and elevating goal that unifies and challenges the team. The same can be said of successful *individuals*: they are driven by clear and elevating goals.

Ted Williams, the legendary Boston Red Sox left-fielder, is considered to be one of the greatest hitters in baseball. He led the league in batting 6 times, won the coveted Triple Crown[139] twice, hit 521 career home runs, and finished with a career batting average of .344. Inducted into the Baseball Hall of Fame in 1966, Williams was the last player to hit over .400 in a season (.406 in 1941), and his .481 on-base percentage is the best in the history of the game.[140]

Like many great athletes, Williams was motivated to succeed by a very specific goal:

The 1-on-1 Development Plan™

A man has to have goals — for a day, for a lifetime — and that was mine, to have people say, "There goes Ted Williams, the greatest hitter who ever lived."[141]

Unlike many athletes, Williams' goal was more than a dream or a grandiose idea. He attacked the idea of becoming baseball's greatest hitter with a passion often attributed to the greatest athletes in sports. In a 2002 article for the Boston Globe, sportswriter Bob Ryan described Williams' devotion to hitting:

Williams studied hitting as if he had been assigned to the Manhattan Project. It is frightening to think what he could have been in the era of videotape, because he was so far ahead of everyone in his day simply by using his five senses. Nothing about either hitting or pitching escaped him, and nothing was deemed too trivial. He studied pitchers. He studied umpires. He studied wind patterns. He was even credited with pioneering the use of rosin, mixing the powder with olive oil to make a sticky substance that predated pine tar by about 10 years.[142]

Williams wanted to become the greatest hitter who ever played baseball—a grandiose dream if there ever was one—but he didn't stop there. He created a plan and became fanatically disciplined to the execution of that plan. His dream became a tangible objective, and his actions were driven by the achievement of that goal.

1-on-1 Principle™: Specific goals are critical to performance improvement, but a goal is only a dream until it is written, reviewed, and measured.

How to Set Goals

Although much has been written about the power of goal-setting, too few people have captured their goals on paper and used them to drive performance. Many people believe that they have established goals when, in reality, all they really have are hopes or dreams. Goal-setting is a very specific process and, when done properly, will lead to distinct improvements in performance.

Terry Orlick, author of *In Pursuit of Excellence* and a sports psychology consultant to hundreds of Olympic athletes, identifies the following keys to successful goal-setting:[143]

- Goals must be specific and measurable.
- Goals must be achievable.
- Goals must be broken into manageable pieces.

Goals must be specific and measurable

The first step in setting goals is to be *specific* about the goal and to *define the measurements* that will allow the employee to know when the goal is reached.

Ted Williams had to translate his vision of becoming the best hitter in baseball into something tangible, which, for him, was baseball's Triple Crown—leading the league in batting

The 1-on-1 Development Plan

average, home runs, and runs-batted-in (RBIs). Only 2 players, Williams and Rogers Hornsby, have won the Triple Crown more than once, but amazingly, Williams narrowly missed 2 others. In 1941, he topped the league with a .406 batting average and 37 home runs, but finished with 120 RBIs—second behind the Yankee's Joe DiMaggio (125). In 1949, Williams hit a league-leading 43 homers and was tops in RBIs with 159, but finished second in batting average to Detroit's George Kell. The difference between the 2 hitters—.34275 for Williams and .3429 for Kell—was a single hit either way![144]

Was it goal-setting or was it simply talent? Without question, it was both, but enormous talent is often wasted without a goal to provide purpose and focus.

> "When I was growing up (in San Diego), I played baseball every day," [Ted William] said. "I hit day and night. People used to say, 'He's a natural.' But I wasn't. I learned you have to practice. Hitting a moving baseball is the hardest thing to do in professional sports."[145]

In the workplace, if an individual employee sets a goal to be "the best" at his or her job, it does not actually become a goal until specific criteria are identified that define "the best." For instance, a salesperson who desires to be the top-ranked salesperson in the company must know what measurements define "top-ranked." It might be gross sales or profitability or achieving an annual sales target. It might be a combination of those things. However, the desire to be the top salesperson in the company is like wanting to be the best hitter in the major leagues—it must be defined and measured.

Goals must be achievable

An important aspect of goal-setting is to set goals that are achievable, but goals must also stretch individual performance. Goals that are too easy provide little motivation for an individual to push to the limits of their potential, but a goal that is unachievable or too difficult to attain can lead to giving up and a loss of confidence. For many baseball players, the goal to be the "greatest hitter that ever lived" is far from realistic; for Ted Williams, it was completely in line with his talent and work ethic.

Marshall Goldsmith addressed the issue of realistic goals in an article entitled "Helping People Achieve Their Goals":

> Successful people are not afraid of challenging goals—they just need to understand the true commitment that will be required to reach these goals. In fact, clear and specific goals that produce a lot of challenge—when coupled with a realistic assessment of the roadblocks to overcome in achieving these goals—can produce consistently strong long-term results. The benefits of well-thought-out goal setting are clear.[146]

As we discussed in chapter 6, performance often improves in direct proportion to someone's expectation. Great coaches and managers set the bar high for talented team members, but not so high that the goal is unattainable.

The 1-on-1 Development Plan™

Goals must be broken into manageable pieces

To be effective, goals must be broken into manageable pieces. For Ted Williams, to be the best hitter in baseball history is an admirable *overarching goal*; one that is even specific and measurable. For instance, he might have set his sights on breaking the record for the highest career batting average in Major League Baseball history held by Ty Cobb (.366). However, a ten- or fifteen-year goal is hardly motivating and fairly unrealistic. It is far more reasonable to set a goal to lead the league in hitting during a particular year or to aspire to win the Triple Crown that year.

On another level, to be the best hitter in baseball, Williams would have to develop several individual skills: hitting specific pitches (a fastball, a curve, or a slider, for example), hitting pitches in various parts of the strike zone (inside and high, or low and away), laying off pitches outside of the strike zone, pulling the ball to right field, and so on. It would have been entirely feasible to set additional goals each year that addressed those individual skills—a goal for striking out, for example. Reducing strike-outs to a specific objective would be an excellent way of determining efficiency as a hitter.

For an employee, breaking the overall objective into smaller components allows the employee to focus on one thing at a time. Working on smaller, specific skills will help in the achievement of a larger goal. Using a salesperson as an example again, he or she might set objectives for quarterly sales performance rather than annual sales performance. Breaking the long-term annual goal into ninety-day increments makes the objective easier to see.

1-on-1 Management

At the same time, the salesperson can break the overall objective—being the top-ranked salesperson—into *individual* components. This would entail setting specific goals for activities that contribute to the ultimate objective of becoming the top-ranked salesperson. This could include goals for the number of sales presentations given during the quarter, or the number of new contacts made, or the amount of product sold in a certain category.

The 1-on-1 Development Plan™

Written goals are an integral component of the 1-on-1 Development Plan™. Once an employee has defined goals in place, then specific actions can be planned and executed to reach those goals. Developing a team or a company requires a strategic plan, and the same can be said for those employees whose job it is to execute that plan: they need a development plan all their own.

The first step to a successful team is to *identify and hire talent*, but the next step is just as important—to develop that talent as much as possible. In doing so, a manager will often find that employees may have big expectations: they want to make a lot of money, or get a promotion, or develop a new set of skills, for example. Rarely, however, have they committed those objectives to paper along with a specific plan to accomplish them. Until those goals are committed to paper, with a time frame assigned to them and appropriate performance measures identified, they are not goals; they are simply dreams.

Sadly, in many cases, employees wants to achieve something important, but they aren't willing to do what must be done to

The 1-on-1 Development Plan™

be successful. They aren't willing to practice. They aren't willing to fail. They aren't willing to improve. They aren't willing to be disciplined. They aren't really willing to make a serious commitment to the goal.

It is much more common, I believe, to find that people simply haven't been trained to set goals and they don't know *how* to go about developing a plan for success. This is where a great manager can have an enormous impact on an employee—implementing a 1-on-1 Development Plan™. [Note: If you would like a free form specifically designed for the 1-on-1 Development Plan™ plan, you can download one at www.1-on-1Management.com.]

This process is quite simple to implement. The power is actually in the commitment to, and the consistent execution of, the process. Here it is, in a nutshell:

1. Jointly determine employee strengths and weaknesses.

2. Record employee objectives, short-term and long-term, and break them into smaller, measurable, specific goals.

3. Create specific plans for attaining those goals, including any necessary training or instruction.

4. Review goals on a quarterly basis, and revise if necessary.

As with the 1-on-1 Meeting™, employee development is a process that takes time, but again, the pay-off is enormous. Your employees will come to realize that they have a partner in their success. The trust that they develop in your leadership, and the influence that you will have on them, will be enormous.

Identify Strengths and Weaknesses

Any good plan starts with a firm understanding of the current situation. In the case of an individual employee, the current situation includes his or her strengths and weaknesses. What does he or she do well? What areas need improvement? What specific skills need to be developed? As the manager, you should have a firm grasp on the skills and competencies that the employee should possess in order to excel in his or her job. As you observe the employee's performance over time, you will gain a more complete understanding of what areas need to be addressed through training or mentoring.

Record Specific Goals and Create a Plan

Talented employees almost always have aspirations to assume increasing levels of responsibility, take on more complex projects, increase their compensation, or climb the corporate ladder. In other words, they are motivated to achieve certain objectives, and it is your job to know what those things are. Once those objectives are known, you can work with them to establish manageable short-term goals (six months to one year) and long-term goals (one to three years).

For example, an employee may want to become known as a subject matter expert (SME) on a specific software application and, in the process, earn a promotion to a supervisory position on a particular team. In addition to mapping out the necessary training for the software application, it is important to determine the employee's strengths and weaknesses relative

The 1-on-1 Development Plan™

to supervising personnel, leading a team, taking on responsibility, and other critical competencies. Once a plan has been established, it can be reviewed and updated quarterly.

Coaching legend Paul "Bear" Bryant led Alabama to six national championships and fourteen Southeast Conference titles, and a record of 232-46-9. In thirty-eight years of coaching, Coach Bryant had exactly one losing season. In 2007, he was voted as the most influential person in the seventy-five-year history of the SEC.[147] His coaching philosophy was quite successful:

"If you want to coach, you have three rules to follow to win. One, surround yourself with people who can't live without football. Two, recognize winners. And three, have a plan for everything."[148]

Hire winners; hire talent; and *have a plan for everything*—including a specific plan for developing the skills of each one of your employees.

Review Performance Quarterly

The traditional "performance appraisal" routinely produces a significant amount of apprehension for both the employee *and* the manager, and for good reason. Using a rating scale to score an employee's performance on a once-a-year basis is not only ill-advised, it is nonsensical. How is a manager supposed to recap 2,080 hours of work in a single one-hour session? Often with little or no feedback during the course of an entire year,

1-on-1 Management

an employee finds the prospect for a promotion or pay increase encapsulated in this short meeting. This process is not effective, nor is it fair to anyone involved.

Tom Coens and Mary Jenkins, authors of *Abolishing Performance Appraisals*, are convinced that the performance review process is flawed and ineffective:

> . . . let us say it is our fervent belief that appraisal does not work. It impedes the reception of feedback, and there is no solid evidence that it motivates people or leads to meaningful improvement. Due to inherent design flaws, appraisal produces distorted and unreliable data about the contribution of employees.
>
> Too often, appraisal destroys human spirit and, in the span of a 30-minute meeting, can transform a vibrant highly committed employee into a demoralized indifferent wallflower who reads the want ads on the weekend.[149]

Coens and Jenkins cite considerable research indicating that performance appraisals are grossly inadequate and frequently fail to produce the intended results. By way of contrast, "performance review" in the 1-on-1 Development Plan™ is not at all about rating or scoring an employee's performance or behavior; it is about comparing actual work performance to the goals established by the employee. In fact, it is more accurately described as a *goal review* rather than a performance review. It is a collaborative effort to identify any barriers or bottlenecks that may be preventing an employee from accomplishing career goals, whether long-term or short-term.

―――――― The 1-on-1 Development Plan™ ――――――

While specific goal review is suggested to take place on a consistent quarterly basis, ongoing review of employee performance is integrated directly into the 1-on-1 Meeting™ (see chapter 10). This makes the quarterly goal review a natural extension of the ongoing feedback that takes place inside that meeting.

Conclusion

Colin Powell, former chairman of the Joint Chiefs of Staff and former United States Secretary of State, has said, "There are no secrets to success. It is the result of preparation, hard work, and learning from failure."[150] I believe this is a fair assessment, and it identifies three possibilities for failure:

- The failure to prepare (no plan).

- The failure to work hard (no commitment).

- The failure to learn from failure (no accountability).

Neither you nor your employees will reach the pinnacle of success without a good plan, a strong commitment to its execution, and a willingness to learn from the inevitable failures that will arise. The 1-on-1 Development Plan™ allows you to create a growth plan for each employee and substitute real career development for the flawed, and mostly ineffective, performance review.

1-on-1 Insights™

- Collaborate with your employees to establish specific, measurable goals. Without a target to shoot at, you can't define success or measure progress.

1-on-1 Management

- Set the bar high for your employees, but not so high that failure is certain. Goals should challenge, but not discourage.

- If you use an annual performance review, the chance that it is creating more harm than good is almost certain. Reviewing a year of performance in an hour is patently unfair, unreasonable, and unreliable. A consistent review—a quarterly *goal* review supported by frequent one-on-one meetings—is an extremely effective way to detect and improve performance issues.

What Every Great Manager Knows That You Don't

Management without leadership is like tactics without strategy

> "Leadership: The capacity and will to rally people to a common purpose together with the character that inspires confidence and trust."
>
> —Field Marshall Bernard Montgomery

As a consultant, I am often asked to "fix" what is wrong with an organization's *employees*. The specific challenge might be poor performance, little or no accountability, or a perceived lack of commitment to the company. The visible symptoms could be high employee turnover, low employee morale, incessant finger-pointing, or inconsistent job performance. Whatever the case, my response is almost always the same: "Let's talk about your managers."

The reality is that the majority of performance issues are ultimately created by poor managers. As I said in chapter 2, leadership defines an organization. When two out of three managers are considered to be poor leaders, it is absolutely no

1-on-1 Management

surprise that many companies are struggling with performance and turnover issues.[151]

John Maxwell has written several books about leadership and influencing people. One of my favorites is *Winning with People*. In the chapter entitled "The Number 10 Principle," he revisits a presentation he made almost twenty years earlier called "Five Things I Know about People." I'm convinced that these are five things that every great manager learns about people as well:

1. Everybody wants to be somebody.

2. Nobody cares how much you know until they know how much you care.

3. Everybody needs somebody.

4. Anybody that helps somebody influences lots of bodies.

5. Somebody today will rise up and become somebody.[152]

These five concepts are simple, yet incredibly powerful. For some reason, managers tend to forget these basic ideas about human nature—as if the natural responses of people are somehow suspended at work. Employees want to be valued, and they will do their best work for someone who cares about them, helps them, and provides the opportunity for them to rise up and become somebody.

So, what is it that great managers know that you don't?

- They know that effective management is much more about people than process.

- They know that high performance begins with hiring talented employees.

What Every Great Manager Knows That You Don't

- They know that talented people won't work for ineffective leadership.

- They know that managers must create a work environment that encourages top performance.

- They know that all great managers are focused on developing the potential of every employee.

- They know that effective management is done one-on-one.

These are the values that drive 1-on-1 Management™. Great managers know that they are responsible for leading a group of people, and success will accompany the great manager that develops the *group's* potential, not just his or her own potential. They also realize that if a manager adopts the idea that "If you want something done right, you have to do it yourself," the team or the company is limited in performance by what the manager is capable of.

The Drive-By Manager

As I mentioned in the introduction, the ideas and concepts presented in 1-on-1 Management™ are not new or revolutionary; instead, they encapsulate a number of tried and proven real-world techniques practiced by great managers for many years.

In 1982, Tom Peters and Robert Waterman authored the business best-seller, *In Search of Excellence*, which introduced a style of management they refer to as "management by walking (or wandering) around" or MBWA.[153] MBWA is exactly what

1-on-1 Management

you might envision it to be: walking around your department, interacting with employees, asking questions, and encouraging or coaching when possible. Their research on "excellent" companies, completed over twenty-five years ago, discovered—surprise!—that successful companies place a premium on the value of employees:

> Treat people as adults. Treat them as partners; treat them with dignity; treat them with respect. Treat them—not capital spending and automation—as the primary source of productivity gains. These are fundamental lessons from the excellent companies research. In other words, if you want productivity and the financial reward that goes with it, you must treat your workers as your most important asset.[154]

So, why don't more companies treat workers as their most important asset? Frankly, many companies *think* they do. They believe that paying a little higher wage, offering a more complete benefit package, celebrating employee birthdays at work, or offering flex-time is the equivalent of putting people first. Certainly, these types of things are important in the workplace. After all, who doesn't want to make more money or have better benefits? However, as we have discovered, people want to be valued, appreciated, listened to, and empowered to do great work.

As we have discussed, many managers are simply not prepared or trained to value and develop people; instead, they tend to adopt the management style they have seen or experienced before. Not infrequently, it is a command-and-control style; one that is in stark contrast to the 1-on-1 Management™ approach. It

What Every Great Manager Knows That You Don't

is a style of management that I call "drive-by management"—a kind of "hit-and-run" for the workplace.

Practitioners of drive-by management make decisions and tell employees what to do—after all, that is what managers are for, to be in control and in charge. This is most likely the style of management they have worked under in the past and it may be the only frame of reference they have for management practices. As they gain confidence in the position, these managers often observe that employees are not as committed or as responsible as they should be. Sadly, these employees often do not seem to pay close attention to detail or do things exactly right.

Consequently, these managers begin to practice drive-by management in a more serious way. They begin to believe that, "If you want something done right, you have to do it yourself." They frequently have to tell their employees how to complete a task or which project detail should be taken on next. Although they may have once been in favor of "empowerment" as an *employee*, they begin to understand why it probably doesn't work very well after all—it is just too hard to find good employees.

As full-fledged *Drive-by Managers*, they become increasingly frustrated because a fair amount of time is being chewed up each month with the hiring and training of new employees. Commitment and creativity is seemingly non-existent, and the Drive-by Manager is forced to micro-manage the smallest details for most every employee. Stressed to the max, the Drive-by Manager becomes convinced that there is never enough time in the day—certainly not enough time to encourage anyone or recognize the few things that are done well—not even enough time to provide sorely needed training.

1-on-1 Management

In fact, Drive-by Managers are rarely with an employee long enough to observe the injuries their hit-and-run style leaves behind. Quick with a criticism or a correction, the Drive-by Manager must move on to other pressing issues. They often have little notion of the pain their victims feel.

We've all seen the symptoms. You have probably worked for one of these managers. The scenario above may even be a mirror reflection of your own experience. The direct evidence that Drive-by Management is the standard practice in your company is high employee turnover, low morale, and increasing levels of disengagement.

We have probably all worked for a Drive-by Manager, but it is extremely important to recognize that *employers often create or perpetuate this style of management* by failing to adequately train their managers to lead and develop employees. *In the absence of training, most managers will resort to acting the way they think managers should act*—telling people what to do, managing details, and making sure everything is done their way.

Conclusion

Talented employees have become *the* competitive advantage in the workplace. Rarely is a company truly differentiated by anything other than what its people are capable of. The mistake made by most companies is in believing that those employees are the weak link in the productivity chain.

They could not be more wrong.

The weakest link in the chain is the one that connects the boardroom to the stock room. C-level executives or owners

What Every Great Manager Knows That You Don't

create the company's business strategy, but it is the middle manager that puts it into play and oversees its execution by the employees. Any manager that is incapable of hiring, developing, and retaining talented employees is the link that can cause your company to falter or even fail.

By becoming a 1-on-1 Manager™, you will not only increase your team's productivity and performance, you will gain a reputation as a manager that actually understands how to develop people. Peter Drucker, considered "the greatest management thinker of the last century"[155] by GE's Jack Welch, said this about the role of developing people:

> "It's one thing for a company to take advantage of long-term freelance talent or to outsource the more tedious aspects of its human resources management. It's quite another to forget, in the process, that *developing talent is business's most important task*—the sine qua non of competition in a knowledge economy."[156]

When you become skilled as a 1-on-1 Manager™, you, my friend, will become one of your company's most important assets.

Congratulations!

Summary of 1-on-1 Principles™

- Employees join companies, but they quit managers.

- Organizations will directly reflect the values and personality of the leader.

- Employees are human beings. They never lose the need to feel valued, to be recognized, and to be encouraged.

- Developing employee performance and capability is a one-on-one process.

- Poor communication creates the majority of workplace issues.

- Communication is much more than words; it includes your actions, the way you do things, and the things you *don't* do.

- To maximize work performance and ensure job satisfaction, the expectations of the manager and employee must be mutually understood.

- In a positive work environment, employees will rise to the level of the manager's expectations.

- Employees will not exert maximum performance for a manager (or company) that they do not trust.

- Talented employees want to be a part of something special; they want to play on a winning team.

- A manual full of rules is a poor substitute for hiring employees with good character and treating them well.

- Employee empowerment is a process that is completely contingent upon trust.

- The actions of a manager primarily determine the employee's level of engagement and commitment to the company.

- Team success is a function of the development and coordination of individual players.

- Effective people management requires a significant change in how you invest your available time.

- Specific goals are critical to performance improvement, but a goal is only a dream until it is written, reviewed, and measured.

1-on-1 Meeting™ Tips

1) Design the meeting to be about the employee:

    - The meeting is an opportunity for the employee to provide input, ask questions, ask for help, or clarify understanding.

    - There are no "bad" or "wrong" questions from the employee.

    - Use questions to uncover issues or get information regarding problems.

2) Short, weekly meetings:

    - Thirty- to sixty-minute meeting.

    - Initial meetings may be longer; subsequent meetings may be as short as thirty minutes.

    - List specific items that you need additional information on or you want to update—progress on a new account; status of project, etc.

1-on-1 Management

- Review previous week's key activities and objectives.
- Preview this week's activities and objectives—assign new tasks or activities as necessary.
- Plan and prioritize—set expectations, determine critical "next steps."

3) Identify needed resources to complete tasks or projects:

- Agree on needs.
- Agree on time frames.
- Provide written confirmation of resource delivery by e-mail.

4) Communicate and review your expectations:

- Assess performance monthly or quarterly rather than once annually.
- Make sure employees understand your expectations.
- Make sure employees understand what constitutes "excellence."
- Make sure employees know exactly how they are being graded.
- Do not gloss over performance issues!

5) In recognizing mistakes, ask questions:

- What happened?
- What would you do differently?
- How do we correct this problem?
- How do we avoid similar challenges in the future?

6) Praise and encourage:

- Recognize that employees who are attempting to grow will make mistakes.
- How a manager views failure impacts the way the team deals with failure.
- Make recognition personal, specific, and meaningful.

7) Coach:

- Probe with questions.
- Dig deep; discover attitudes.
- "What do you think needs to be done?"
- Review performance to create accountability and responsibility.
- Do not gloss over performance issues; be firm yet supportive.

8) Ask for employee feedback to improve your own performance:

- What can I stop doing?
- What can I start doing?
- What do I need to keep doing?

Appendix A

17 Essential Books for the Great Manager

Branham, Leigh. *The 7 Hidden Reasons Employees Leave: How to Recognize the Subtle Signs and Act Before It's Too Late*. New York: Amacom, 2005.

Buckingham, Marcus and Curt Coffman. *First, Break All The Rules*. New York: Simon & Schuster, 1999.

Collins, Jim. *Good to Great: Why Some Companies Make the Leap . . . and Others Don't*. New York: Harper Collins, 2001.

Connors, Roger, Tom Smith, and Craig Hickman. *The Oz Principle: Getting Results through Individual and Organizational Accountability*. New York: Prentice Hall, 2004.

Covey, Steven R. *The 7 Habits of Highly Effective People*. New York: Simon and Schuster, 1989.

Covey, Stephen R. *Principle-Centered Leadership*. New York: Simon and Schuster, 1992.

Drucker, Peter F. *Classic Drucker*. Boston: Harvard Business School Press, 2006.

Gostick, Adrian and Chester Elton. *The Carrot Principle*. New York: Free Press, 2007.

Kotter, John P. *Leading Change*. Boston: Harvard Business School Press, 1996.

Kouzes, James M. and Barry Z. Posner. *Encouraging the Heart: A Leader's Guide to Rewarding and Recognizing Others*. San Francisco: Jossey-Bass, Inc., 1999.

Lencioni, Patrick. *The Five Dysfunctions of a Team—A Leadership Fable*. San Francisco: Jossey-Bass, 2002

Maister, David H. *Practice What You Preach: What Managers Must Do to Create a High Achievement Culture*. New York: Free Press, 2001.

Maxwell, John C. *Winning with People*. Nashville: Thomas Nelson, 2004.

Maxwell, John C. *The 21 Irrefutable Laws of Leadership*. Nashville: Thomas Nelson, 1998.

Patterson, Kerry, et al. *Crucial Conversations: Tools for Talking When Stakes are High*. New York: McGraw-Hill, 2002

Rath Tom and Donald O. Clifton. *How Full is Your Bucket?* New York: Gallup Press, 2004.

Schwarzkopf, H. Norman. *It Doesn't Take a Hero*. New York: Bantam, 1992.

Notes

Introduction

1. Brown, Tom et al. *Business Minds: Management Wisdom, Direct from the World's Greatest Thinkers*. Financial Times Prentice Hall, 2001. Page 150.

2. Quote taken from David Maister's video "On Managing: Train a Pigeon", available at *Maister Moments: David Maister Live*. <http://davidmaister.com/videocast/412/>.

Chapter 1: The Path to Management

3. "Management." *Wikipedia: The Free Encyclopedia*. <http://en.wikipedia.org/w/index.php?title=Management&oldid=139238401>.

4. "U.S. Job Satisfaction Keeps Falling, The Conference Board Reports Today." *The Conference Board*. February 28, 2005.

5. Goleman, Daniel. *Emotional Intelligence*. Bantam: New York, 1995.

6. Goleman, Daniel, Richard Boyatzis, and Annie McKee. *Primal Leadership: Realizing the Power of Emotional Intelligence*. Boston: Harvard Business School Publishing, 2002. 62.

7. For a good example of this type of text, see Stephen P. Robbins and Mary Coulter's *Management* (8th Ed. Prentice Hall: Upper Saddle River, NJ, 2005).

8   For a list of books that I would consider indispensable to any great manager, see Appendix A.

9   Mintzberg, Henry. *Managers, Not MBAs: A Hard Look at the Soft Practice of Managing and Management Development.* 2003, Berrett-Koehler, San Francisco, CA.

10 Vogl, A.J. "Managerial Correctness." *The Conference Board Review* (July/Aug 2004): 2.

11 Ibid. 2.

Chapter 2: Workplace Challenges

12 "Influence." *Merriam-Webster Online Dictionary*. Merriam-Webster, Incorporated. <http://www.merriam-webster.com/dictionary/influence>.

13 "U.S. Job Satisfaction Keeps Falling, The Conference Board Reports Today." *The Conference Board.* February 28, 2005. <http://www.conference-board.org/utilities/pressDetail.cfm?press_ID=2582>.

14 "Major Workforce Study Exposes Serious Disconnects Between Employers and Employees." *Spherion 2005 Emerging Workforce Study*. Spherion Corporation. 2005. <http://www.spherion.com/press/releases/2005/Emerging_Workforce.jsp>.

15 Bartlett, Christopher A. and Ghoshal, Sumantra. "Building Competitive Advantage through People." *MIT Sloan Management Review.* 2002 (43): 35.

16 Colvin, Geoffrey. "Catch a Rising Star." *CNNMoney Fortune.* (January 30, 2006). <http://money.cnn.com/magazines/fortune/fortune_archive/2006/02/06/8367928/index.htm>.

Notes

17   "Leading Expert Says Businesses Must Plan Now For Dramatic Skilled Labor Shortage by 2010." *RushPRnews*. August 2, 2006. <http://rushprnews.com/labor-shortage-press-release-08022006.html>.

18   Buckingham, Marcus and Curt Coffman. *First, Break All The Rules*. New York: Simon & Schuster, 1999. 33.

19   Collins, Jim. *Good to Great: Why Some Companies Make the Leap . . . and Others Don't*. New York: Harper Collins, 2001. 72.

Chapter 3: What Employees Really Want at Work

20   Byrne, John A. "How Jack Welch Runs GE: A Close-up Look at How America's #1 Manager Runs GE." *Business Week* (June 8, 1998). The McGraw-Hill Companies, Inc. <http://www.businessweek.com/1998/23/b3581001.htm>.

21   Ibid.

22   "SHRM Job Satisfaction Series: 2005 Job Satisfaction Survey Report." *Society for Human Resource Management*. June 2005.

23   "Giving Employees What They Want: The Returns Are Huge." *Knowledge@Wharton*. May 4, 2005. University of Pennsylvania. <http://knowledge.wharton.upenn.edu/article.cfm?articleid=1188>.

24   "SHRM Job Satisfaction Series: 2005 Job Satisfaction Survey Report." *Society for Human Resource Management*. June 2005.

25   Leplante, Alice. "MBA Graduates Want to Work for Caring and Ethical Employers." *Stanford Graduate School of Business Research*. January 2004. Stanford Graduate School of Business. <http://www.gsb.stanford.edu/news/research/hr_mbajobchoice.shtml>.

26 "Do You Know Your Worker Wants?" *Foreman Facts.* (Labor Relations Institute, New York), December 5, 1946.

27 The study done by the Labor Relations Institute of New York was replicated with similar results by Lawrence Lindahl (1949), Ken Kovach (1980); Valerie Wilson, Achievers International (1988); Bob Nelson, Blanchard Training & Development (1991); Sheryl & Don Grimme, GHR Training Solutions (1997-2001).

28 Murray Jr., Michael R. and Warren L. Strickland. "Managing for growth: An interview with former Emerson CEO Chuck Knight." *McKinsey Quarterly.* (November 2006). McKinsey & Company. <http://www.mckinseyquarterly.com/article_page.aspx?ar=1876&L2=18&L3=30&srid=17&gp=0>.

29 Wheatley, Margaret. "Goodbye, Command and Control." *Leader to Leader.* (July 1997). Margaret J. Wheatley. <http://www.margaretwheatley.com/articles/goodbyecommand.html>.

30 Ibid.

Chapter 4: Introduction to 1-on-1 Management™

31 "Gallup Study: Engaged Employees Inspire Company Innovation." *Gallup Management Journal.* (October 12, 2006). The Gallup Organization. <http://gmj.gallup.com/content/24880/Gallup-Study-Engaged-Employees-Inspire-Company.aspx>.

32 "Career." *The Official Website of George "The Gipper" Gipp.* Estate of George Gipp. <http://www.cmgww.com/football/gipp/biography.htm>.

33 "Biography." *The Official Website of George "The Gipper" Gipp.* Estate of George Gipp. <http://www.cmgww.com/football/gipp/biography.htm>.

Notes

34 Howald, Emily. "Win One for the Gipper." *Scene—Observer Online*. January 17, 2003. The University of Notre Dame. <http://www.nd.edu/~observer/01172003/Scene/0.html>.

35 "The Big Games". *The Official Athletic Site of the University of Notre Dame*. The University of Notre Dame. <http://www.cstv.com/auto_pdf/p_hotos/s_chools/nd/sports/m-footbl/auto_pdf/FBRecSuppBigGames>.

36 "Biography." *The Official Site of Knute Rockne*. Estate of Knute Rockne.
<http://www.knuterockne.com/biography.htm>.

37 Wagner, Rodd, Aleksander Wawer, and James K. Harter. "A Manager's Revolutionary Idea at International Paper." *Gallup Management Journal*. August 10, 2006. The Gallup Organization. <http://gmj.gallup.com/content/23950/3/A-Managers-Revolutionary-Idea-at-International.aspx>.

38 Hamm, John. "The Five Messages Leaders Must Manage." *Harvard Business Review*. 84 (May 2006): 116.

39 Gostick, Adrian and Chester Elton. *The Carrot Principle*. New York: Free Press, 2007.

40 Rath, Tom and Donald O. Clifton, Ph.D. How Full Is Your Bucket? *Positive Strategies for Work and Life*. New York: Gallup Press, 2004.

Chapter 5: Effective Communication in the Workplace

41 *Columbia Accident Investigation Board Report*. National Aeronautics and Space Administration. Limited First Printing. August 2003. 49. <http://anon.nasa-global.speedera.net/anon.nasa-global/CAIB/CAIB_lowres_full.pdf>.

42 Ibid. 177.

43   Ibid. 187.

44   Ibid. 195.

45   Caplan, Jeremy. "Cause of Death: Sloppy Doctors." *Time.* (January 15, 2007). Time, Inc. <http://www.time.com/time/health/article/0,8599,1578074,00.html>.

46   Mehrabian, A. *Silent Messages: Implicit Communication of Emotions and Attitudes*. Belmont, CA: Wadsworth, 1981.

47   "Legacy of the Riots: 1992-2002; Charting the Hours of Chaos." *Los Angeles Times*. April 29, 2002. <http://pqasb.pqarchiver.com/latimes/access/116901306.html?dids=116901306:116901306&FMT=ABS&FMTS=ABS:FT&type=current&date=Apr+29%2C+2002&author=&pub=Los+Angeles+Times&edition=&startpage=B.6&desc=LEGACY+OF+THE+RIOTS%3A+1992-2002%3B+Charting+the+Hours+of+Chaos>.

48   Delk, James D. *Fires & Furies*: The L.A. Riots. Palm Springs, CA: ETC Publications, 1995. Pages 221-222.

49   Kotter, John P. "Leading Change: Why Transformation Efforts Fail." *Harvard Business Review*. (March/April 1995). Rpt. in *Harvard Business Review* 85 (January 2007): 100.

50   LaBarre, Polly. "The Agenda—Grassroots Leadership." *Fast Company Magazine*. 23 (March 1999). Mansueto Ventures, LLC. <http://www.fastcompany.com/magazine/23/grassroots.html>.

51   Abrashoff, D. Michael. "Retention Through Redemption." *Harvard Business Review*. # (February 2001).

52   LaBarre, Polly. "The Agenda—Grassroots Leadership." *Fast Company Magazine*. 23 (March 1999). Mansueto Ventures, LLC. <http://www.fastcompany.com/magazine/23/grassroots.html>.

53   Ibid.

Notes

54 Covey, Stephen. *The 7 Habits of Highly Effective People*. New York: Simon and Schuster, 1989.

55 Peck, M. Scott. *The Road Less Traveled: A New Psychology of Love, Traditional Values and Spiritual Growth.* New York: Touchstone, 1978.

Chapter 6: The Power of Expectations

56 "Yogi Berra Quotes." *Thinkexist*.
<http://thinkexist.com/quotes/yogi_berra/>.

57 "Determining System Inadequacies Responsible for Human Error." *Army Accident and Investigation Reporting*. Department of the Army. November 1, 1994. 22.
<http://www.army.mil/usapa/epubs/pdf/p385_40.pdf>.

58 Kannapel, Patricia J. and Stephen K. Clements, et al. *Inside the Black Box of High-Performing High-Poverty Schools: A Report from the Prichard Committee for Academic Excellence*. Prichard Committee For Academic Excellence. February 2005.
<http://www.prichardcommittee.org/Ford%20Study/FordReportJE.pdf>.

59 Ibid.

60 Ibid.

61 Ibid.

62 Livingston, J. Sterling. "Pygmalion in Management." *Harvard Business Review*. 47 (1969).

63 "Johann Wolfgang von Goethe Quotes." *Thinkexist*.
<http://thinkexist.com/quotes/johann_wolfgang_von_goethe/4.html>.

64 "SEAL Challenge Contract Instructions." *Official U.S. Navy SEAL Information web site*. Naval Special Warfare Command.
<http://www.seal.navy.mil/seal/contractinstructions.aspx>.

65 "Navy SEALs Special Operations Training." *BaseOps Network*. <http://www.baseops.net/basictraining/navyseals/warningorder.html>.

66 de Koning, Guido M.J. "Evaluating Employee Performance (Part 1)." *Gallup Management Journal*. The Gallup Organization. November 11, 2004.
<http://gmj.gallup.com/content/default.aspx?ci=13891&pg=1>.

67 de Koning, Guido M.J. "Evaluating Employee Performance (Part 2)." *Gallup Management Journal*. The Gallup Organization. December 9, 2004.
<http://gmj.gallup.com/content/14209/Evaluating-Employee-Performance-Part-2.aspx>.

68 Ibid.

69 Ibid.

Chapter 7: Four Key Questions Every Manager Must Answer (Part 1)

70 "WorkUSA® 2002 – Weathering the Storm: A Study of Employee Attitudes and Opinions." *Watson Wyatt Worldwide*. 2002. <http://www.watsonwyatt.com/research/resrender.asp?id=W-557&page=2>.

71 Ibid.

72 Kotter, John P. *Leading Change*. Boston, MA: Harvard Business School Press, 1996.

73 Schwarzkopf, H. Norman. *It Doesn't Take a Hero*. New York: Bantam, 1992. 169.

74 Cannon, Jeff and Jon Cannon. *Leadership Lessons of the Navy Seals*. New York: McGraw-Hill, 2003. 92.

Notes

75. Hamm, John. "The Five Message Leaders Must Manage." *Harvard Business Review.* 84 (May 2006). 116.

76. Larson, Carl and Frank LaFasto. *Teamwork: What Must Go Right, What Can Go Wrong.* Newbury Park, CA: Sage Publications, 1989. 27.

77. Cannon, Jeff and Jon Cannon. *Leadership Lessons of the Navy SEALS.* New York: McGraw-Hill, 2003. 100.

78. Banks, Don. "Complacent? No way: Belichick, Patriots back to work at Friday's minicamp." *Sports Illustrated Online.* (April 29, 2005). Time, Inc. <http://sportsillustrated.cnn.com/2005/writers/don_banks/04/29/pats.minicamp/index.html>.

79. Greenberg, Alan. "Belichik Game Plan for Life." *Hartford Courant.* (May 3, 2004). <http://www.allthingsbillbelichick.com/articles/2004/gameplan.htm>.

80. Brown, Clifton. "Lions Fire Mariucci and Promote Jauron." *The New York Times.* (November 29, 2005). <http://www.nytimes.com/2005/11/29/sports/football/29detroit.html>.

81. Foster, Terry. "Losing Set in Mind of Lions." *The Detroit News.* (January 02, 2007). <http://www.detnews.com/apps/pbcs.dll/article?AID=/20070102/SPORTS0101/701020321/1004/SPORTS>.

82. Stack, Jack. *The Great Game of Business.* New York: Doubleday, 1992.

83. "Fire team." *Wikipedia: The Free Encyclopedia.* <http://en.wikipedia.org/wiki/Fireteam>.

Chapter 8: Four Key Questions Every Manager Must Answer (Part 2)

84 "Band of Brothers." DreamWorks/SKG (2001). Directed by David Frankel and Tom Hanks. Based on the novel, *Band of Brothers*, by Stephen Ambrose.

85 Hill, Tom. Presentation. *Character Training Institute*. Oklahoma City, OK. February 28, 2006.

86 Washington, Booker T. *Up from Slavery: An Autobiography*. New York & Co.: Doubleday, 1901. Accessed online from the chapter entitled "Making Their Beds Before They Could Lie on Them." <http://www.bartleby.com/1004/11.html>.

87 Cannon, Jeff and Jon Cannon. *Leadership Lessons of the Navy SEALS*. New York: McGraw-Hill, 2003. 88.

88 Buckingham, Marcus and Curt Coffman. *First, Break All the Rules*. New York: Simon & Schuster, 1999. 27.

89 Ibid. 28.

Chapter 9: Creating An Environment of Employee Engagement

90 Branham, Leigh. *The 7 Hidden Reasons Employees Leave*. New York: Amacom, 2005. 27.

91 Ibid. 3.

92 Ray, Barry. "Who's afraid of the big bad boss? Plenty of us, new FSU study shows." (December 4, 2006). <http://www.fsu.com/pages/2006/12/04/BigBadBoss.html>. Research to be published: Harvey et al. "Dealing with bad bosses: The neutralizing effects of self-presentation and positive affect on the negative consequences of abusive supervision." *Leadership Quarterly* (in press).

Notes

93 "Engaged Employees Inspire Company Innovation." *Gallup Management Journal.* (October 12, 2006).
<http://gmj.gallup.com/content/24880/Gallup-Study-Engaged-Employees-Inspire-Company.aspx.>.

94 Branham, Leigh. *The 7 Hidden Reasons Employees Leave.* New York: Amacom, 2005. 19.

95 Pacetta, Frank and Roger Gittines. *Don't Fire Them, Fire Them Up.* New York: Fireside, 1994. 26.

96 Ibid. 14.

97 "Biography." *Official web site of Frank Pacetta.*
<http://www.frankpacetta.com/bio/default.cfm>.

98 Schwarzkopf, H. Norman. *It Doesn't Take a Hero.* New York, NY: Bantam, 1992. 153.

99 Ibid. 152.

100 Kouzes, James M. and Barry Z. Posner. *Encouraging the Heart: A Leader's Guide to Rewarding and Recognizing Others.* San Francisco: Jossey-Bass, Inc., 1999. 4.

101 Gostick, Adrian and Chester Elton. *The Carrot Principle: How the Best Managers Use Recognition to Engage Their People, Retain Talent, and Accelerate Performance.* New York: Simon & Schuster, 2007. 16.

102 "Compilation of Turnover Cost Studies." *Sasha Corporation.* January 2007.
<http://www.sashacorp.com/turnframe.html>.

103 Kouzes, James M. and Barry Z. Posner. *Encouraging the Heart: A Leader's Guide to Rewarding and Recognizing Others.* San Francisco: Jossey-Bass, Inc., 1999. 91.

104   Gostick, Adrian and Chester Elton. *The Carrot Principle: How the Best Managers Use Recognition to Engage Their People, Retain Talent, and Accelerate Performance.* New York: Simon & Schuster, 2007. 116.

105   Amabile, Teresa M. and Steven J. Kramer. "Inner Work Life: Understanding the Subtext of Business Performance." *Harvard Business Review.* 85 (May 2007). 83.

106   Collins, Jim. *Good to Great: Why Some Companies Make the Leap . . . and Others Don't.* New York: Harper Collins, 2001. 13.

Chapter 10: The 1-on-1 Meeting™

107   Kindred, Dave. "An extraordinary Joe." *The Sporting News.* (November 2, 1998).
<http://findarticles.com/p/articles/mi_m1208/is_n44_v222/ai_21251723>.

108   Useem, Jerry and Lisa Munoz. "A Manager for All Seasons." *Fortune.* (April 30, 2001).
<http://money.cnn.com/magazines/fortune/fortune_archive/2001/04/30/301967/index.htm>.

109   Ibid.

110   Abrashoff, Michael D. "Retention through Redemption." *Harvard Business Review.* (February 1, 2001).
<http://harvardbusinessonline.hbsp.harvard.edu/hbsp/hbr/articles/article.jsp?ml_action=get-article&articleID=R0102L&ml_page=1&ml_subscriber=true>.

111   Ibid.

Notes

112 Wagner, Rodd Aleksander Wawer, and James K. Harter. "A Manager's Revolutionary Idea at International Paper." *Gallup Management Journal*. The Gallup Organization. 2006.
<http://gmj.gallup.com/content/23950/3/A-Managers-Revolutionary-Idea-at-International.aspx>.

113 "Ken Blanchard Quotes." *Thinkexist*.
<http://thinkexist.com/quotes/ken_blanchard/>.

Chapter 11: Coaching in the Workplace

114 "Profile: Duke's Winning Coach Isn't Afraid of Losing." *CNN/Time*.
<http://www.cnn.com/SPECIALS/2001/americasbest/TIME/society.culture/pro.mkrzyzewski.html>.

115 "Opening Round: Dayton Practice Day Quotes." *Official web site of the NCAA*. March 15, 2004. Note: Quote from Florida A&M head coach Mike Gillespie, Sr. Florida A&M played Lehigh in the NCAA tournament "play-in" game for the final spot in the 2004 NCAA basketball tournament.
<http://www.ncaasports.com/basketball/mens/story/7180610>.

116 Coach Krzyzewski led Duke to a 9-3 record in 1994-95, but was forced to leave the team early in the season for health issues that included back surgery and exhaustion. The Blue Devils finished the season with a 13-18 record.

117 John Wooden (10), Adolph Rupp (4), and Bob Knight (3)

118 Coach K's accomplishments are detailed at <http://www.coachk.com>, <http://www.goduke.com/>, and <http://en.wikipedia.org/wiki/Mike_Krzyzewski>.

119 "Profile: Duke's Winning Coach Isn't Afraid of Losing." *CNN/Time*.
<http://www.cnn.com/SPECIALS/2001/americasbest/TIME/society.culture/pro.mkrzyzewski.html>.

1-on-1 Management

120   Gregory, Sean. "The Way of K." *Time Magazine*.
      <http://www.time.com/time/magazine/article/0,9171,1226165-2,00.html>.

121   "Coach K Quotes." *Coach K: The Official web site of Coach Mike Krzyzewski*.
      <http://www.coachk.com/quotes.php>.

122   Lonnie White. "NBA Stars Sold on Team USA's Coach K." *Los Angeles Times*.
      <http://www.latimes.com/sports/la-sp-ushoops20aug20,1,6067227.story?coll=la-headlines-sports>.

123   Goleman, Daniel, Boyatzis, Richard, and Annie McKee. *Primal Leadership: Learning to Lead with Emotional Intelligence*. Boston: Harvard Business School Press, 2004. 62.

124   "Larry Coker Profile." *Official Athletic Site of the Miami Hurricanes*.
      <http://hurricanesports.cstv.com/sports/m-footbl/mtt/coker_larry00.html>.

125   Collins, Jim and Jerry I. Porras. *Built to Last*. New York: Harper Collins, 1994. 170.

126   "Fortune selects Henry Ford Businessman of the Century." *Time Warner*. Press Release, November 1, 1999.
      <http://www.timewarner.com/corp/newsroom/pr/0,20812,667526,00.html>.

127   Welch, Jack and Suzy Welch. "How to Be a Good Leader." *Newsweek*.
      <http://www.msnbc.msn.com/id/7304587/site/newsweek/page/0/>.

128   "2001 Annual Report." *General Electric Company*.
      <http://www.ge.com/annual01/letter/page7.html>.

129   "Professional Recognition of Marshall Goldsmith." *Marshall Goldsmith Library*.
      <http://www.marshallgoldsmithlibrary.com/html/marshall/recognition.html>.

Notes

130 Lyons, Laurence S. "Coaching at the Heart of Strategy." *Coaching for Leadership: How the World's Greatest Coches Help Leaders Learn*. Eds. Marshall Goldsmith, Laurence Lyons, and Alyssa Freas. San Francisco: Jossey-Bass/Pfeiffer, 2000. 6.

131 Goldsmith, Marshall. "Coaching for Behavioral Change." *Coaching for Leadership: How the World's Greatest Coches Help Leaders Learn*. Eds. Marshall Goldsmith, Laurence Lyons, and Alyssa Freas. San Francisco: Jossey-Bass/Pfeiffer, 2000. 21.

132 "Vince Lombardi Quotes." *Brainy Quote*. <http://www.brainyquote.com/quotes/quotes/v/vincelomba130743.html>.

Chapter 12: The 1-on-1 Development Plan™

133 "Rocky Balboa." *Box Office Mojo*. <http://www.boxofficemojo.com/movies/?id=rocky6.htm>.

134 Rocky (1976). Written by Sylvester Stallone and directed by John G. Avildsen. Distributed by United Artists and MGM.

135 Ibid.

136 "Mark Price." *Wikipedia, The Free Encyclopedia*. <http://en.wikipedia.org/w/index.php?title=Mark_Price&oldid=163343568>.

137 "Mark Price." *Basketball Reference*. <http://www.basketball-reference.com/players/p/pricema01.html>.

138 "Quotations by Robert Heinlein." *The Quotations Page*. <http://www.quotationspage.com/quotes/Robert_Heinlein/>.

139 In baseball, the Triple Crown is achieved when a player leads the league in batting average, home runs, and runs batted in (RBIs).

1-on-1 Management

140 "Ted Williams." *Official web site of Major League Baseball.* <http://mlb.mlb.com/mlb/news/tributes/mlb_obit_ted_williams.jsp>.

141 Ryan, Bob. "His Desire Made Wish Come True." *The Boston Globe.* July 5, 2002. <http://www.boston.com/sports/redsox/williams/stories/his_desire_made_wish_come_true.shtml>.

142 Ibid.

143 Orlick, Terry. *In Pursuit of Excellence: How to Win in Sport and Life Through Mental Training.* Champaign, IL: Human Kinetics, 2000.

144 Schwartz, Larry. "Williams left a legacy of greatness." *ESPN.com.* (July 5, 2002). <http://espn.go.com/classic/obit/williams_ted_moments.html>.

145 Dan Schlossberg. "Ted Williams: he mastered the strike zone." *Baseball Digest.* (March 2002). < http://findarticles.com/p/articles/mi_m0FCI/is_3_61/ai_82472897>.

146 Goldsmith, Marshall and Kelly Goldsmith. "Helping People Achieve Their Goals." *Leader to Leader Magazine.* 39 (2002).

147 "SEC's Most Influential: The Top 25." *The Birmingham News.* <http://blog.al.com/bn/2007/07/secs_most_influential_the_top.html>.

148 "Bear Bryant Quotes." *ThinkExist.* <http://thinkexist.com/quotes/bear_bryant/>.

149 Coens, Tom and Mary Jenkins. *Abolishing Performance Appraisals: Why They Backfire and What to Do Instead.* San Francisco: Berrett-Koehler, 2000. 17.

150 "Colin Powell Quotes." *ThinkExist.* <http://thinkexist.com/quotes/colin_powell/>.

Notes

Chapter 13: What Every Great Manager Knows that You Don't

151 Press Release. "U.S. Job Satisfaction Keeps Falling, The Conference Board Reports Today." *The Conference Board.* February 28, 2005.

152 Maxwell, John. *Winning with People: Discover the People Principles That Work for You Every Time.* Nashville, TN: Thomas Nelson, Inc., 2004. 101.

153 Peters, Thomas J. and Robert H. Waterman. *In Search of Excellence: Lessons from America's Best-Run Companies.* New York: Warner, 1982. 121.

154 Ibid. 238.

155 "The Man Who Invented Management: Why Peter Drucker's Ideas Still Matter." *BusinessWeek.* (November 28, 2005). <http://www.businessweek.com/magazine/content/05_48/b3961001.htm>.

156 "The Man Who Invented Management: Why Peter Drucker's Ideas Still Matter." *BusinessWeek.* (November 28, 2005). <http://www.businessweek.com/magazine/content/05_48/b3961001.htm>.

About the Author

Kelly Riggs is the founder and president of Vmax Performance Group, a business performance improvement company located in Broken Arrow, OK. Widely recognized as a powerful speaker and dynamic trainer in the fields of leadership, sales development, and strategic planning, Kelly is a Registered Corporate Coach (RCC) with the World Association of Business Coaches. He has spent the last twelve years teaching and training organizational leaders in sales and executive management, and his passion is developing people-focused managers and high-performance salespeople.

Since forming Vmax in 2006, Kelly has provided leadership training for the University of Oklahoma JCPenney Leadership Center, been selected as the leadership trainer for the Oklahoma Associated General Contractors and Constructor's Leadership Council, and appeared before a subcommittee of the Oklahoma State House of Representatives to address *Factors That Impact Employee Engagement and Performance.*

Kelly is currently working on his second book, *1-on-1 Selling™: How to Win More Sales, Defend Your Margins, and Build Your Brand,* to be published in 2010.

For more information, email kelly@vmaxpg.com or visit www.1-on-1Management.com